AF691553

CHRIS DAEMS

The right of Chris Daems to be identified as the
Author of the Work has been asserted by him in accordance
with the Copyright, Designs and Patents Act 1988.

Copyright © Chris Daems 2026

Editor: Shaun Russell

ISBN: 978-1-918097-72-6

Published by
Jelly Bean Books
Mackintosh House
136 Newport Road, Cardiff, CF24 1DJ
www.candyjarbooks.co.uk

All rights reserved.
No part of this publication may be reproduced, stored in a retrieval system, or transmitted at any time or by any means, electronic, mechanical, photocopying, recording or otherwise without the prior permission of the copyright holder. This book is sold subject to the condition that it shall not by way of trade or otherwise be circulated without the publisher's prior consent in any form of binding or cover other than that in which it is published.

Reader Reviews

"This book is a vital resource for any founder navigating the complex emotional landscape of exiting a business. It perfectly articulates the 'Identity Void' many of us face, moving beyond the financials to address the profound question of 'Who am I without my company?' The focus on stewardship and legacy resonates deeply with my work; it doesn't just discuss the transaction, it honours the human transition.

I believe this is a useful resource for all business founders who are contemplating something other than just the golf course or travel. Chris is a very human and accessible guide with lots of practical tips to help anyone in creating their next chapter."

Alex Keay – Founder, Succession Plan Coach

"A genuinely valuable guide for people sitting on the edge of a major life transition."

Ian Price

"*What Happens Next* is just the kind of guide you wish you had before retirement sneaks up on you. Practical, grounded, and full of smart tools, it helps you reimagine what life could look like and then actually take action to live it that way. A brilliant companion for designing your next chapter."
Justin Walton – Executive Coach, Financial Wellbeing Specialist

"It's a great read, and takes you on a journey of experience, storytelling and thoughtfulness, delving into the softer, human side of financial planning."
Jamie Jenkins

"Chris is one of the rare financial planners who understands that money is only one of many ingredients you need to fund a long and meaningful life. He shows that wellbeing, purpose, social connections, and vitality matter as much as any investment portfolio.

This book is a wonderful insight into how Chris helps you framework your life. Forget the giant leap: he uses insights from ancient philosophy, modern financial psychology, and 'Design Thinking' to show you how to start running small, low-risk experiments today to build the life you want to live."
Tom Mathar

"This is a very practical and thought-provoking book, especially for anyone at the stage of life when they might be thinking about retirement or even that they should think about retirement. It upends all the assumptions about what that stage of life should look like, asking probing questions and providing useful frameworks like NEXT for navigating the changes of this stage of life. There are many helpful insights, particularly around purpose and identity but it always comes back to the question,

so what are you going to do about it? Highly recommended and I would give it to my clients."
Hilary Rowland

"Chris, and *What Happens Next*, approaches the subject of retirement from a refreshing angle; acknowledging the importance of money while identifying the equal importance of the other factors which make we humans flourish: purpose, connections, health, and feeling part of something. An accessible, actionable and humorous must-read for anyone planning their 'What Happens Next'."
Ruth Sturkey – Business Coach, former Chartered Financial Planner and Chair of the Institute for Financial Wellbeing

"This book came at just the right time for me. As someone designing the next stage of their life, 'What Happens Next' opened my eyes to a more holistic approach that considers not just my career but all aspects of my wellbeing. It brings structure, real-life stories and practical tools to help you understand where you are today and how to explore what's next. Written with humour, empathy and practicality, it's a great companion to guide you!"
Graham Alldis

"I started with the intent of choosing one or two key points of feedback, but quickly realised that I was identifying an illuminating or at least highly relevant point every two to three pages!

The real-life case studies brought so much context to the associated chapters, and I will absolutely refer to the Kübler-Ross change curve model often. Put simply, although entirely

different, *What Happens Next* – like *The Kindness Project* – is an entirely unique read and an absolute must for the progressive individual to hold dear in the literary collection!"
Louise McNamee

"First and foremost, I really enjoyed the book. Chris has such an engaging style of writing and for me the clear message is that we all have (or can create) opportunities to design the life we want to live. In an ever-changing world where the definition and nature of 'retirement' is completely different to how it was viewed perhaps even just twenty years ago; we also have the ability to shift course and redesign our lives if we plan early enough.

Some elements reminded me of *The 4-Hour Workweek* by Tim Ferriss where he talks about fear-setting, having mini-retirements during our working lives and testing out our hobbies before fully committing to them. The central theme of planning your life before life makes a plan for you is a key reminder for all of us that time is the most valuable commodity we have."
Paul Forde

Contents

Contents

Chapter One

The Story of Mike

'Retirement is not the end of the road. It is the beginning of the open highway.' – Unknown

On January 3rd, 2023, a client sent me the strangest message I've ever received. There was no explanation, no greeting, just a photograph of a box.

On the box was a photo of a World War II German fighter plane. If you know anything about German fighter planes, which I don't, you might have recognised that it was a Messerschmitt.

The reality is that I know as much about German fighter planes as I know about how to perform brain surgery, juggling chainsaws or parenting a teenager.

In fact, had I not known better, my first guess would be that Messerschmitt was some sort of German sausage dish. Like Currywurst but better.

However, the fact that the box had Airfix printed on the side, along with a photo of the plane itself, clarified its contents.

So I know what you're wondering...

Why Have I Been Sent a Photo of a Box Containing the Model of an Old Plane?

The photo came from Mike, a client of ours for about six months. Mike was a senior engineer in a large car business. We'd worked with several of his colleagues in the past, and one of them kindly told Mike it was probably worth us having a chat.

I believe that no one chooses to see a financial planner for fun. It's typically because they've reached a stage in their lives where they want to make sure they are making the right decisions and need help to move in the right direction.

Ultimately, though, when you spend a decent amount of time with a client, they always want the answer to one clear question.

Have I Got Enough?

The definition of 'enough' is different to each client. For some, this means planning how to pass their assets to their children. For others, it's about whether there's still enough time for what's ahead. But for Mike, and for many like him, enough meant something very different.

'Chris,' he began, 'I know you've done this for a few colleagues, and friends of mine as clients, and I'd like you to help me too...'

'Okay, how do you think I can help?' I asked.

'I'd like to know whether I've got enough money to never worry about working again.'

Normally, it takes a while before clients raise this. Mike, on the other hand, had been referred to us by someone we'd previously supported – and he was clear about what he wanted.

I wanted to understand what had triggered the change...

'Why have you decided to look at this now, Mike?' I asked.

'I've been in my job for over three decades, Chris, and whilst I still enjoy bits of it, there are elements which frustrate me every day. There are massive benefits in working for a big organisation, but I'm not doing things I like as much. I might moan about it, but enough is enough, and I need to make a change. Can you help me with this?'

I love having conversations with clients about time and how they spend it. I then asked Mike what he would do if he didn't work.

'Oh, I've got loads to do in the house, Chris,' he replied. 'Jobs I've been putting off for ages, and of course I'd walk the dog!'

'How about after that?' I asked, wondering how many jobs he'd been putting off, and how many times he could actually walk his dog.

'I'll cross that bridge when I come to it,' Mike told me.

'Okay,' I said. 'If you need me, let me know.'

Now, Mike is a lovely guy with an acerbic wit and a very dry sense of humour. It's one of the reasons I like him. So I shouldn't have been surprised when I eventually received the text accompanying the image for the model aeroplane.

Mr Daems, this is what retirement has become. Perhaps I need to get out more?

The dry humour in the comment made me chuckle. Still, it also made me wonder whether Mike actually was okay – so I called him. He seemed to be doing well, though I sensed something was missing.

Perhaps he needed to get out more. Perhaps he needed a plan for life, not just money. Perhaps retirement needs rethinking altogether.

However, while I could have spent time concentrating on what Mike should do, my focus changed to something different. What could *I* do to help?

I'm proud of the work we do at Cervello.

Helping people get clarity on their financial decisions – so they can live well, provide fairly for the next generation, and feel supported along the way – is work I'm proud of.

Financial wellbeing is a fundamental part of overall wellbeing. So helping people understand where they stand financially, and what they need to do next, is at the heart of what we do.

I know that the work I do with clients as a Chartered Financial Planner has a positive impact. Otherwise, I wouldn't do it. It's as simple as that.

The challenge I often face is my curiosity. Sometimes I wish I could switch this off – just to give my family and friends a break from my constant questions. But I can't help thinking how we help people weigh everything that matters when they're trying to figure out what *enough* really is.

Questions like...

- If we know we've got enough money, does that equip us to live the next few decades with high levels of wellbeing?
- How do we advise on life if we're all 'built' differently with varying needs, desires and wants?
- What is a life well lived? What is success, particularly in our later lives?
- How do we decide, after decades of building a business or working in a senior position in a business?

What Happens Next?

To answer this question, I drew on my own knowledge, and I got curious. I read loads of books, many of which I will recommend along the way. I asked my clients about their greatest successes, challenges, hopes, dreams, fears, desires and blocks.

I also interviewed a wide range of experts on subjects including money, purpose, awe, work, nutrition, sleep, and much more. I put every single one of these interviews and all of my insights on YouTube.

Here's my one-line take on all the research I've completed...

Working out your own version of *What Happens Next* is nuanced and complex. You should not only think about money, but purpose, wellbeing, relationships, and your most finite resource – particularly as we hit a certain point in our lives - time.

I can't offer all the solutions you need, but I'm confident that the insights, thinking models and frameworks shared in this book will be helpful.

Of course, I'm also conscious that the journey is yours, not mine. This book has, very simply, been written to help.

I often joke that the reason I've written this book is to help me in the not-so-distant future. I must admit I've learned a lot about the challenges we face in our fifties and sixties when planning the next chapter of our lives.

In reality, I have a good understanding of how to successfully transition into 'retirement'. I'm not there myself yet, but still believe that the thousands of hours I've spent helping clients like you (as well as reading widely, reflecting deeply and interviewing loads of experts) will help you navigate the next chapter of your life. It's the only reason I've written this book. For people like you (or Mike).

I remember a client, his face tinged with melancholy, saying, 'Everybody looks at my life and tells me I'm successful. But after all these years of climbing, I can't help wondering if my ladder is leaning up against the right building.

I'm writing this book for anybody whose business or career might still deliver some satisfaction, but it's not the same as it once was.

On most days, you recognise how incredibly grateful you are to live the life you do, and with most points, you're almost certainly correct. However, you increasingly feel something that is missing, and you have no clear roadmap for what happens next.

Added to this, you're not entirely convinced that the conventional 'retirement' is right for you. You want more freedom for travel and relaxation, but you also recognise you've still got a lot to give.

This is why so many people just carry on. The alternative, the so-called 'ideal' retirement we're often told to aspire to – spending our days on a bench overlooking a beach – can feel equally terrifying. It reminds us that we still have so much to give.

The Problem with the Conventional Model of Retirement

America, 1860. A young entrepreneur found himself reflecting on his previous failed business. The original idea felt good. Abraham Lincoln was the presidential nominee and was growing in popularity. The young man, Milton Bradley, printed and sold an image of Abraham Lincoln, and initially, the business was incredibly successful. However, Abraham Lincoln did one thing which scuppered Milton's chances of initial success.

He grew a beard.

You see, Milton's prints were printed before Lincoln decided to grow the beard. People complained and demanded their money back, and Milton's stock of photos of beardless Lincoln suddenly had no value. Who knew that facial hair could result in the demise of someone's fledgling business!

However, not to be deterred by this initial failure, and inspired by an imported board game his friend had given him, Milton moved on to the project which would launch him into success.

Milton, in 1860, invented, published and sold his first board game...

The Game of Life

At the time, the game looked different to the multi-coloured affair we see today. It was originally called *The Checkered Game of Life* and was played on what can only be described as a sepia chessboard, with messages on every other square.

Some squares included barriers, which would hold you back from the game, which included 'Prison' and 'Ruin'. Other squares meant you won points. These included 'Going to College' (five points), 'Wealth' (ten points), and the maximum number of points you could gain was by reaching 'Happy Old Age' (fifty points).

It's unclear whether fifty was the number of points you gained by reaching 'Happy Old Age', or whether fifty was seen as old at the time. Admittedly, life expectancy at the time was just over thirty-eight, so I wouldn't be surprised if in the 1880s, fifty was considered ancient.

Milton's game evolved over time. The boards became bigger and more colourful. The aim of the game changed when the modern version was released in 1960. Instead of gaining points, you now accumulate as much money as possible.

This version of the game, with a few small tweaks along the way, has remained the one many of us played and still play.

I love *The Game of Life*. It's a brilliant way to spend a couple of hours. But there's one thing that particularly interests me. The game stops when you retire. You've won when you stop. Also, the only definition of success is how much money you've accumulated by the end... and that's the crux of the problem.

Now, I know *The Game of Life* is only a board game, and clearly the actual game of life is a lot more nuanced and complicated than could ever be expressed with a big piece of colourful cardboard and a few bits of plastic.

However, I do find myself reflecting on the model of 'success' presented in the game, and how our ancestors saw their lives through the industrial age, and into our modern lives.

Only recently have we seen these lives in three phases: We learn, we earn, and then what? We rest? How appealing does that sound to you?

Of course, we might want a little rest, but most of us want a lot more than that. Interestingly, prior to the Industrial Revolution, the three broad life stages didn't exist. In the UK, most people learned informally at home, with compulsory education not existing until the late nineteenth century. In human terms, it's a relatively new concept.

So why did these three stages of life become the norm very quickly? The answer is complicated.

In reality, during the industrial age, this model worked remarkably well for a rapidly changing world. Governments gained a more literate, numerate population and, as industry expanded, a larger workforce from which to raise taxes. For individuals, education became more accessible, and factory work meant greater security and stability than farming ever could.

And...

It really worked for employers.

Factories and the corporations that owned them benefited from a workforce that was already partially trained and ready to work, having been educated and conditioned for work in schools.

Industrial-age employers also gained from retirement becoming the norm. This allowed businesses to replace older workers with younger ones.

So over the past two hundred years, the three-stage life model mostly worked. You learned, you earned your money, and then, after years of intense and often very physical labour, you stopped work and relaxed.

But does this work for us humans in the early twenty-first century? I'm not convinced. Here are a few reasons why...

Firstly, we're all living longer.

When the first state pension was introduced, by renowned German statesman and owner of one of history's most impressive moustaches, Otto von Bismarck in 1889, it paid people from the age of seventy, when the average German lived until their early forties. Today, according to the Office for National Statistics, if you're a UK-based female and sixty today, you're likely to live until the age of eighty-seven on average, with a 25% chance of living until ninety-five, and a one in sixteen chance of living until one hundred.

Now, in many developed countries, we may live two, three and potentially four decades past the traditional 'finish line'. That's a long time to simply rest, particularly if we're only resting on that bench overlooking the beach.

Secondly, the nature of work has fundamentally changed.

Many of us are no longer doing back-breaking manual labour. Instead, knowledge, creativity, and relationships matter more than physical stamina. For some, that means they want (or need) to keep working long after any fixed retirement age.

Thirdly, we need to rethink retirement, because work today is bound up with identity, meaning, and purpose.

In the past, community, religion, or family offered a strong sense of who they were outside work. Today, work often plays a bigger role in how we define ourselves. To simply stop can feel like stepping off a cliff.

And finally, we're not satisfied with 'just enough'. We want our later lives to be rich with purpose, contribution, joy, connection, and, yes – fun. The old three-stage model doesn't make space for that.

So perhaps the real question isn't 'Have I got enough?' but 'Enough for what?'

Enough to live well. Enough to give. Enough to feel a sense of purpose. Enough to still be curious about the future.

Redefining Retirement

There's also a reason that I've not used the word 'retirement' in the title of this book. Simply, I don't think it fairly reflects what so many of us, probably including you, want to do when we reach our fifties and sixties, and want to make a change in our lives.

You see, the word retire is French in origin, with the original meaning to 'withdraw', and even today, the Merriam-Webster dictionary defines retirement as...

Withdrawal from active working life.

Or...

A place of seclusion.

Or...

Withdrawn from one's position or occupation, having concluded one's working or professional career.

For me, all these concepts are appetising as the food celebrities eat in the *I'm a Celebrity...* jungle each year. I think I'll stick with my wife's amazing cooking and avoid the concept of withdrawing from life, even when I reach the point of thinking about 'what's next'.

There are plenty of useful books that share useful tips about a successful 'retirement'. However, in this book, I want you to broaden your horizons when it comes to thinking about our future.

I want to empower you to think about your 'potential' future. I want you to be excited about what happens next.

For many of my clients, and maybe for you, it's likely that the coming few decades may bring a change in focus from the way time was spent earlier in life.

We can call this retirement. We can call it 'What Happens Next'. We can even call it Steve. Or Alan.

However, regardless of the thing we used to call 'retirement', my experience is that the change can often be tough, with new pressures, challenges and concerns.

Firstly, for most people in their mid-fifties to early sixties, the kids have grown up. While they may not be entirely independent, financially or otherwise, the level of dependence on Mum and Dad is often, though not always, reduced.

One factor that can weigh heavily on some of my clients – and I'm seeing this more and more – is that their parents may need continued care.

Secondly, as we age, there's certainly an increased focus on our mortality. While there are certainly plenty of amazingly healthy individuals in their later lives, we reach an age where the clock starts to tick a little bit louder.

Thirdly, an increased awareness of mortality makes us more reflective. We ask more questions and, if work no longer fulfils us, the pressure to change begins to build.

My clients have typically had successful work lives. They've achieved a degree of financial security and success, and this increased period of self-reflection has often led to a realisation that they might want to do something else with their time.

This change can be exciting. However, it can also be scary, difficult to get used to, and prepare for.

Often, in my experience, the change people want to make in their fifties and sixties is about finding passion, purpose, and living lives linked to their values. It's about looking at financial wellbeing and making sure you can afford to move on.

It's about staying intellectually engaged while continuing to do things you enjoy. This is about you! If you are stepping away from your current business or occupation, it's worth thinking about what work gives you in terms of social wellbeing, and how you might recreate that.

It's about your place in your community, and it's about protecting your own health throughout the next phase of our lives.

This book is written with the people I help every day in mind. People like you.

However, one thing I don't want to do is overpromise and underdeliver. This book clearly isn't a panacea for all of the challenges you face when we're thinking about the next chapter of your life. Also, I want one thing to be clear before we start...

This book is a toolbox. It's a toolbox of ideas, questions and stories. Some of these ideas will help you work out 'what happens next', but some (for you personally) might be less effective.

Some of the questions I ask you will challenge you, and you may have the answers to others. Some of the stories will resonate; others may not.

I'm happy to promise one thing, though. There will be a decent amount in this book, which I'm confident will help you in the next five to ten years.

If there's not, get in touch, and I'll refund the cost of the book and throw in a Curly Wurly for good measure.

There's a great quote I read the other day which sums up the challenge of working out your best 'what happens next'...

Every complex problem has a solution. A solution which is simple, direct, plausible... and also wrong.

Like most things in life, working out your ideal retirement (or What Happens Next, or Steve!) if you're at a crossroads, won't be a simple solution.

It won't be a straight line. You won't get the same answer to 'what's next' for you by following someone else's model, or even someone else's advice.

What might help, however, is simply reading widely, getting help if you need it, speaking to people who have gone through their own 'what happens next' moments, and taking the ideas that you believe might work for you...

...and trying stuff.

The truth is, you're unlikely to feel comfortable about what's next until you try things you've never done before and see if they truly fit.

I've tried my best to ask some insightful questions, share the insights of people who have gone through the experience, and provide some exercises I know will make the path a little bit clearer.

In reality, a change in our lives might be necessary, but it isn't always easy, particularly if it involves thinking deeply about your purpose, exploring aspects of your wellbeing, and embracing your inner child.

In the pages ahead, I invite you to explore the question for yourself. Not through the narrow lens of money alone, but through the wider lens of wellbeing, purpose, and time.

Because the truth is this: the old model of retirement no longer works for most of us.

And if you agree with me that this is true, we must ask the question anew – *what happens next?*

Let me start, in the next chapter, by sharing some of the frameworks and ideas you can use to start to work towards the ideal next stage of your life.

Chapter Two

Why Frameworks are Vital for Your What Happens Next Journey

'Plans are worthless, but planning is everything.'
– Dwight D. Eisenhower

I was three hours deep, and I was no further forward. I'd annoyed myself, and for the last thirty minutes one recurring thought had kept sneaking back into my head...

'Why have I spent three and a half hours looking for a new padel tennis racquet, and yet I'm still no closer to working out which one might be best?'

You see, after nearly five decades of being on this planet, and having avoided racquet sports for most of my life, I'd recently been enjoying the odd game of padel tennis.

I'd been playing for a few months with a cheap racquet I picked up online, but as I'd started to gradually and incrementally improve, I thought I'd invest in a new one.

Easy, I thought. Do a bit of research. Work out the most

appropriate one and then decide. Big mistake. You see, I was suffering from what Barry Schwartz described in his brilliant book, *The Paradox of Choice*, as 'analysis paralysis '.

The fact that my wife, Cassie, now calls herself a 'padel widow' probably tells you everything you need to know about how many odd games I'm playing. With over one thousand models, all with different shapes, weights, textures, makes and prices, it made this choice virtually impossible. While my padel-related analysis paralysis might be unique to me and other padel playing compatriots, we've all experienced the same feeling. Whether it's spending too much time deciding what to watch on Netflix, or what to order in a restaurant, or planning where to go on holiday, we recognise that increased research time doesn't necessarily help us make these decisions.

Now, imagine extending the analysis paralysis I suffered when buying a new padel racquet, or your last time on Netflix, to the next three to four decades of your life.

In truth, this is a period where we can potentially do anything or everything we want, such as learning Cantonese, taking up pottery, or spending an afternoon pretending to be a unicorn (and I'm assuming you're doing this to entertain the young people in your life, but there's no judgement if you simply enjoy it!)

Often, the choice is so overwhelming that we find ourselves a bit stuck. This, I believe, is why the individuals I speak to often maintain the status quo, despite not being entirely happy with their ongoing careers.

Now, when we're booking holidays, or picking what we want to watch on telly, we normally use mental shortcuts (often called 'heuristics'). It's why choosing a takeaway doesn't take four hours each time. You know what you like, or go for the easiest option. That's a heuristic at work. It's a rule of thumb, which saves us from drowning in the detail.

However, when deciding on the next chapter of our lives, the decisions are far more complex and way more nuanced than deciding between a vindaloo or korma. We can use mental frameworks to help us take positive action and move forward successfully into the next chapter of our lives.

So let's look at the ideas, concepts and frameworks we'll visit and revisit throughout this book while we're planning out your ideal next chapter of life.

A Focus on Wellbeing Not Happiness

When people first hear about the *What Happens Next* project, many assume it's about happier next chapters. After all, who doesn't want to be happier?

However, you'll notice throughout this book we talk a lot less about happiness and a lot more about wellbeing, and there's a science-backed reason why. Simply put, Happiness is fleeting, wellbeing is more sustainable.

Happiness is a temporary emotional state. While happiness is great when it happens, the reality is that nobody is happy all the time.

Wellbeing is a broader and deeper definition than happiness, and a better concept to examine in this book. Wellbeing is about being resilient to stress, having the health and energy to do what you want, feeling life is worth living, alongside connection and belonging... all important concepts we're going to explore in depth in this book.

It's a bit of a paradox, isn't it? The more we chase happiness, the less happy we become. Instead of chasing happiness, we're going to focus on something we can proactively improve – our wellbeing.

So we've built a framework – and we will continue to revisit this throughout the book – which highlights specific areas of wellbeing but also assists us to consider our purpose, values and identity.

A Story, the Research, the Wisdom and the Practice

As I delve into each area of wellbeing, I'm going to start each new chapter with a story. A story designed to illustrate how and why each area of wellbeing is important in the framework of our lives, particularly when we're thinking about managing change.

I'm going to share insights from academic research, ancient and modern philosophy, and the wisdom our expert guests have been generous enough to share on the subject.

Then, we're going to be practical and discuss what we can do to improve our wellbeing when negotiating 'what happens next' in our lives, but also how to keep track of our wellbeing (using the NEXT framework), and how we can get more 'bang for our buck' by stacking our wellbeing.

Rapid Low-cost Experimentation

When you're facing a big life change, stepping away from full-time work, starting a business, or reimagining how to spend the next three decades, it's easy to think you need to make one giant leap into the next chapter of your life.

But often that's the exact mindset that keeps people like you and me stuck. After all, if we're making important decisions about the next twenty to thirty years of our lives, making the right choices is difficult.

In my experience, that's when both the self-doubt and questions kick in.

Questions like...

What if I choose the wrong road to take in the next chapter of my life?
What if I make a big decision and waste time and money?
Or
What if I do something momentous and then regret it!?

However, there is good news. There is a simple concept that can be applied across all aspects of our lives to minimise the cost of decisions (in both time and money), reduce regret, and allow for a swift U-turn if we find ourselves heading down the wrong road.

I first read about 'rapid low-cost' experimentation in the brilliant book *Design Your Life by* Bill Burnett and Dave Evans.

Bill and Dave are experts in a concept called 'design thinking', which is a way to solve problems originally used in business, healthcare, and education, but the tools can also be used to refine the life you want to live.

At its core, the principle is simple. Don't make big decisions about the next chapter of your life in one go. Simply design your life incrementally by running small, low-risk experiments.

Design thinking is rooted in solving problems creatively. Designers don't sit in a room until the 'perfect' idea arrives. They sketch, prototype, test, and iterate. Each step gives them feedback they can build on.

Life design works the same way. It's not necessary to be certain what your ideal retirement, career shift, or purpose looks like. You just need to try something small that moves you closer, and then you see what happens.

Throughout this book, I'm going to share a bunch of rapid low-cost experiments to improve your wellbeing in a number of areas. However, I'd suggest the benefits of rapid low-cost experimentation are threefold.

First, the risk of making a big change is reduced. If we're making small incremental changes towards a big goal, then if we change our mind, we can do it more quickly.

Secondly, taking incremental action gives you more clarity. When you run experiments, even small ones, you discover more about yourself than by thinking or researching endlessly.

Thirdly, small steps are less intimidating. Big steps can feel a bit scarier. However, incremental small steps towards a big goal reduce the fear factor when making big changes.

I recently tried a rapid, low-cost experiment: renting a camper van for a few weeks rather than buying one – a decision that would have involved a far more significant change.

You see, I wanted the adventure of travelling in a camper van, but I wasn't sure if I was suited for permanent van life. It turns out that while we created some great memories travelling around the UK, neither my wife Cassie, my daughters Charlotte and Sophie, or I could see camper vans in our permanent future.

However, and this is the thing about low-cost experimentation, we learned new things about ourselves, which helped inform our future decisions.

This is why it's important to look at the information you get from these experiments as feedback, not failure.

Appreciating the Change Curve

Often the changes we make in our fifties and sixties, while right for us, are some of the biggest changes we make in our lives.

Selling a business is a momentous change. Leaving a decades-long career is another significant milestone. Often, these changes might not be chosen but instead imposed. I'm thinking about redundancy and where your adult kids might still be dependent, but your Mum or Dad might need more help too.

There's been plenty of research on how to cope with change. One such way is by Swiss-born psychiatrist, Elisabeth Kübler-Ross.

Kübler-Ross Change Curve Model

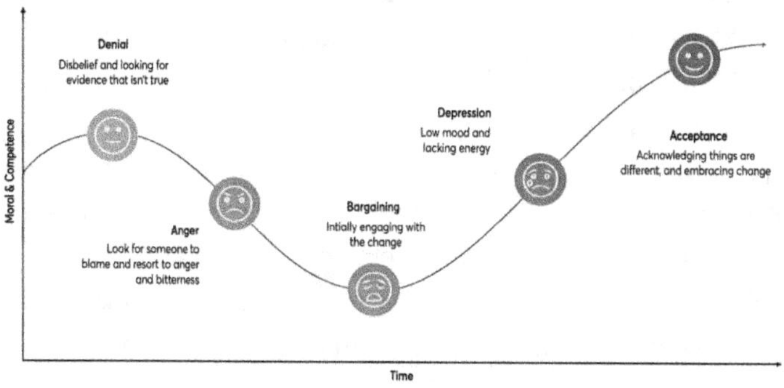

You see, while the process of accepting change is different for all of us – and we may not experience every part of it on the same timescale – it's important to remember that change is a process. As a result, what happens next in your own life may unfold gradually.

That's why I believe that when navigating this change, it's important to be kind to ourselves and understand that there are no wrong or right answers. Your journey will be slightly different from everyone you know (including your mate Steve and your cousin Bob) and you're going to experience a bunch of challenging emotions on the way to accepting any change.

It's also why we'll revisit the change model in future chapters, particularly when we're thinking about the road to 'what happens next'.

Create the Plan. Evolve the plan. Follow the N.E.X.T Process

As a financial planner, I'm constantly talking about the importance of planning. You might be surprised to hear, however, that I'm not a big fan of rigidly sticking to a plan.

Dwight D. Eisenhower said, 'Plans are worthless, but planning is everything.'

I'd also like to quote underrated modern-day philosopher Mr Mike Tyson, who perhaps less eloquently but more directly said, 'Everyone's got a plan until they get punched in the mouth.'

Now, if we're thinking about what happens next in our lives, we shouldn't worry about getting punched in the mouth. However, both Eisenhower and Tyson were right. Planning is important but so is constantly evolving the plan.

The reality is that you'll learn many things on your journey to 'what happens next', but some may change your perspective on what you want to do next. Your perspective may change on what an ideal balance looks like. Your perspective may change as you go through certain stages of later life.

The key here is to build the plan for 'What happens next', but continuously revisit it to ensure it continues to remain relevant for you.

I think the easiest way to think about building a plan is to use the analogy **N.E.X.T.**

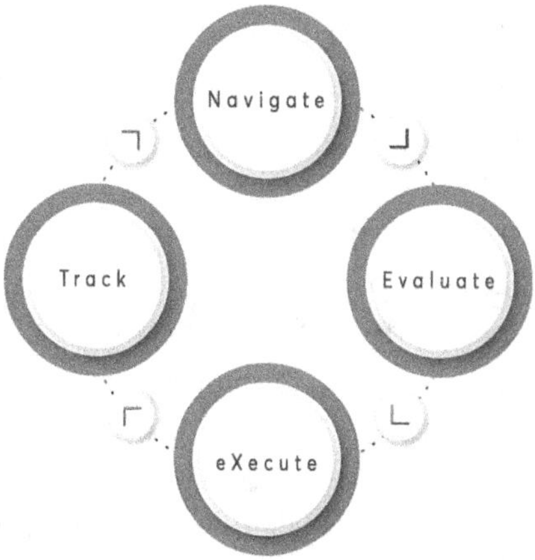

Navigate – Work out where we want to go.
Evaluate – Work out where we are.
eXecute – Take the action to incrementally get to where you want to go.
Track – Check you're still heading in the right direction.

Also, while I'm a firm believer in focusing our time and efforts on what we can control, we also need to accept that things will happen in our lives beyond our control.

I once had a client with whom we worked hard to build a

robust plan, only for him to go through a relationship breakdown and divorce a couple of years later.

For the time it took to go through this, planning for the future wasn't his focus. I kept in touch with him, primarily to make sure he was doing okay, and support him, although he did surprise me one day with the following comment, 'All that planning we did, Chris. It was pointless. Therefore, I've concluded that planning my life in any respect is a bit pointless.'

To be frank, it's not what your financial planner – who if they've done their job right by investing loads of time, effort and energy in building your plan – wants to hear. It's lucky I'm not a particularly sensitive soul!

However, at the time I understood how this particular client felt. The plan we'd built wasn't relevant because of this fundamental change to his life.

I understood and I told him this, 'I get it. I completely understand that all of that planning we did feels pointless and it's not unusual to feel despondent when times are tough. However, can I make a suggestion? Shall we rebuild the plan once you're ready? My experience tells me that the process of planning is more important than the actual plan itself.'

After a few months, I received an email with one line. 'Chris, the dust has cleared and I'm ready to plan again.

While there's plenty you can control when thinking about 'What happens next' there's also loads you can't.

You can't control what the politicians do, so changes in laws and tax rates impacting your life might have an impact on your plan. An illness or accident might have an impact on your plan. You don't know when you might have a family emergency.

Also, we might also change our minds. I've seen so many

times individuals alter their plans as they navigate the first few months of a new chapter of their lives.

As Bobby Brown sang in the late '80s, 'It's your prerogative.' Actually he sang about his prerogative, but that's not important right now.

Over time, particularly as you're learning more about what you really love to do with your time, you might want to change your plan to reflect what you've learned about what you love. These things can and do happen in our lives. That's why we revisit our plans on a regular basis to ensure we course correct, and why building the plan is important, but arguably evolving the plan on a regular basis is fundamental too.

We almost take it for granted, but when I think of the most sophisticated planning tool, I always go back to your route mapping software of choice.

You choose a destination (the navigate stage), your software knows where you are (the Evaluate stage) and then builds you a route towards your destination (**eXecute**).

Despite this, plans change. Bad weather, accidents, traffic, all delaying the most direct route or slowing down progress.

What most navigation systems do is notify you of the delay and look for alternative routes without you needing to worry.

Most of us would never indulge in a decent journey without mapping out our destination, so why wouldn't we work out what we want, work out where we are, work out what we need to do, and re-plan when stuff gets in the way in other aspects of our lives?

Wellbeing Stacking

When most people think about making positive changes to their lives, they imagine tackling each area of wellbeing separately.

You might take one action to improve your fitness, one action to improve your social wellbeing, and another to improve your financial wellbeing. The challenge is if we want to improve and maintain our wellbeing across different areas, it's probably going to feel a bit overwhelming.

That's where the idea of 'wellbeing stacking' comes in.

Wellbeing stacking is the practice of choosing actions that improve multiple areas of your wellbeing at the same time. Instead of treating social, physical, financial, intellectual, and community wellbeing as isolated silos, we look for activities that overlap and deliver compound benefits.

It's inspired by James Clear's work in *Atomic Habits*. Clear describes the idea of 'habit stacking' – building new habits by attaching them to existing ones. For example: 'After I brush my teeth, I will floss one tooth.' It's a way to piggyback new behaviours onto old routines.

Wellbeing stacking takes this principle further. It asks: 'What's one thing I could do that creates a ripple effect across several dimensions of wellbeing?'

I've seen the benefits of wellbeing stacking in my own life. My family and I moved home recently from East London out to a lovely Essex town called Leigh-on-Sea.

We agreed the move would be positive, but I was concerned about the social connections I'd made where I lived before.

At the same time, I decided to take up padel tennis and it filled my social wellbeing bucket. I found myself connecting with new people, building friendships, and sharing plenty of laughs along the way. I'd turn up for a game and build great connections and even friendships with those I played with.

It clearly improves physical wellbeing. Padel is fast, fun, and forgiving on the joints compared to tennis or squash. It gave me the sense of energy and vitality that comes from regular movement.

However, learning a new sport from scratch was also an amazing intellectual challenge and continuing to learn how to become a better player keeps me engaged. I've still got a lot to learn but I'm really enjoying the challenge this gives me.

So a simple thing like taking up padel tennis can enhance various elements of your life, and there are so many ideas that could improve various aspects of your wellbeing.

As we move on, I'm going to be sharing some ideas that help improve wellbeing across a variety of areas of your life. Not grand gestures, but everyday actions you can take so that you're filling your wellbeing bucket in multiple areas at the same time.

However, before we look at each area of wellbeing individually, I want to spend some time looking at your specific why.

Often the initial thing we need to face when we're thinking about the next chapter of our lives is three fundamental questions. Questions which for many of us are incredibly challenging but powerful to answer as a part of the key to unlock a life well-lived.

Chapter Three

Purpose, Identity and Values

'Efforts and courage are not enough without purpose and direction.' – John F. Kennedy

I've had many conversations over the past few years highlighting just how difficult and challenging the transition into the next chapter of our lives, typically in our fifties and sixties, can be. However, there's one that springs to mind time and again.

It was a client we'd worked with several years ago, and who'd achieved his definition of financial independence a couple of years later.

Recently, though, I'd been feeling our meetings had been a little repetitive – like a financial planning version of *Groundhog Day*.

The meetings used to go like this...

First, the client would tell me how he'd stopped enjoying work some years ago. It wasn't that he hadn't achieved success in his work. He was at the top of his own particular game. He was well respected. He was rewarded well financially.

He often told me how grateful he was that a combination of opportunity and hard work had put him in this position. However, after tragically losing both friends and family over the past couple of years, he had also become a little bored – and far more aware that time was the most finite commodity in his life.

Then, I went on to tell him that he was still in a position where, based on the assumptions we'd used to build his plan, I was confident he'd never run out of money. I then asked him how this might inform the decisions he was now going to make.

Every year without fail, he told me the same thing. He'd think about it.

However, every year he'd return in the same position – doing a job he was bored with, knowing that the time to spend on the life he truly wanted to live was ticking away. Frustrated but not taking any action. The last time we had this conversation helped me understand why.

I'd asked him about his dissatisfaction with work every year and why he continued to come, still bored and dissatisfied, and seemingly stuck in this loop where nothing changes.

That's when he looked me in the eye with a melancholy look on his face. 'Chris,' he started, 'I understand I've got enough from a financial perspective and appreciate the work you've done to help me with this. I've been thinking about this a lot, and I think the challenge isn't a financial one. It's more fundamental than that. I know I don't enjoy my work, but who am I without it?'

If you've asked this question of yourself, you aren't alone. Often, the greatest challenge we face when we're thinking about making positive change in our fifties and sixties is how our identity changes, and where purpose comes from in this chapter of our lives.

You see, often when we're in our twenties, thirties or forties, the purpose in our lives comes from our roles. Purpose might come from raising our families and building our careers. However, when your kids are grown and the passion you once had for your work now wanes, where does identity come from in this stage of our lives?

The challenge is that the status quo is comfortable. It's reliable. The new world, where your identity and purpose are in a state of flux, isn't as straightforward. However, I believe there are several things we can do to navigate the potential change in identity, find new purpose and get really clear on the values that underpin it.

When it came to my client, having understood it wasn't about the money, I asked him three questions inspired by the brilliant work of George Kinder. Questions which are difficult to answer but, in my experience, provide real insight.

First, knowing you've got enough money for the rest of your life, what one small thing would you change first?

Secondly, if you knew you only had five years left to live but were in perfect health, how would you choose to spend this time?

And lastly, *if you only had twenty-four hours left, what would you regret not doing?*

My client didn't answer immediately. However, over the next few months, I gradually saw a positive momentum in him.

Basically, I think the route you should consider taking when thinking about 'what happens next' is to revisit what's truly important to you. Your values.

Why is Revisiting and Clarifying Our Values So Important?

Certain decisions in life should be relatively easy. If you're asking whether you should have Marmite on your toast in the morning, the answer is – unless you're some sort of strange individual who actually likes it – probably no.

If you want to know the most underrated part of a Christmas dinner that answer is always Brussels sprouts, while the answer to the best part of any dinner, particularly a festive one, is pigs in blankets.

By the way, if you don't know what a pig in blanket is, I'm sorry, but I don't think we can be friends.

However, there are plenty of decisions which, unfortunately, aren't as easy, but these choices still must be made. Or not. Ultimately, not deciding is still a choice.

It's often the most consequential decisions we make that tend to be the most difficult.

In the scheme of things, it doesn't matter whether you like Marmite or what your favourite part of a Christmas dinner is.

However, there's one big question which is often really difficult to answer...

How Do I Decide How to Spend My Time in this Upcoming Chapter of My Life?

For example, if we've got two opportunities to support a charity as a trustee, which one should we choose?

Or...

How do you decide what job works for you in the next phase of your life? Is it a portfolio career or part-time in one workplace? Or no work at all?

Or...

When and how should you spend time creating memories with the people you love and like?

Or...

How much time should we spend supporting our communities? This is why being clear about our values matters so much. When the choices in front of us feel endless (and let's be honest, in this stage of life, they often do), values act like a compass. They don't give us the map or the turn-by-turn instructions, but they do offer us a general direction to head.

The social scientist Shalom Schwartz mapped universal values across cultures, from security and tradition to achievement and self-direction. His research found that while people's rankings differ, the clearer you are about your own hierarchy of values, the easier it is to make decisions, and the more consistent your life feels.

This matters because transitions are disorienting. One day you're 'Head of X Department,' the next you're just 'Dave' or 'Sharon'.

If your identity is pinned to the role, you wobble when the role disappears. However, if your identity is anchored to values (for example, learning, contribution, or adventure), those can be expressed in multiple ways, regardless of job title.

It's why when people say, 'I don't know who I am without my work,' I gently suggest, 'Perhaps who you are isn't the role, but the *values* that role expresses.' And if that's true, you can find other ways to live those values in your next chapter.

What Ancient and Modern Wisdom Tell Us About the Identity, Purpose and Values Challenge

This isn't a new problem. Ancient philosophers wrestled with the same question: What makes for a life well-lived?

Aristotle spoke of *telos* – a purpose or end that shapes the good life. For him, flourishing came from living in accordance with virtue, not chasing fleeting pleasure.

The Stoics reminded themselves daily that externals could be lost – wealth, jobs, status – but character and chosen action remain ours. As Epictetus put it, 'You are a role, not a title.'

However, the quote that always comes back to me when thinking about purpose and values belongs to Viktor Frankl.

Frankl endured the horrors of the concentration camps in World War II, lost his family, but survived to share his incredible insights. His perspective... 'Those who have a "why" to live can bear almost any "how".' In other words, our values aren't luxuries; they help us cope with change in our lives.

So identifying our values might be our first step.

Modern psychologists and philosophers both agree that having purpose in our lives is fundamentally important to our overall wellbeing.

Ancient philosophers like Aristotle used not to only talk about fun, relaxation and enjoyment being important, but we also need to ensure that we focus on our Eudaimonic wellbeing, which is living with purpose, growth and in line with our values.

Modern researchers like Carol Ryff, Richard Ryan and Edward Deci all studied the importance of values. However, my favourite insights are from Patricia Boyle at Rush University and the fine work done at the University of Michigan.

These studies show that adults with a strong sense of purpose are less likely to experience depression, feel less lonely, and are more physically active. They also have a reduced risk of Alzheimer's disease, better heart health, and greater resilience after illness.

Ensuring we maintain a sense of purpose throughout our lives, therefore, appears vital to living a happy, healthy life with a strong sense of wellbeing.

But what do ancient philosophers and modern-day researchers agree on when it comes to navigating our own identity.

The answer is clear...

Identity is important, but we shouldn't hold on too tightly to a narrow definition of this.

When we tie our entire sense of self to a single role, title, or achievement, we become vulnerable to change. When identity is broader, more flexible, and grounded in our deeper values, it can bend without breaking as life inevitably shifts.

The Stoics, particularly Epictetus, warned that pinning your identity to things outside your control – such as job titles, wealth, or reputation – sets you up for distress.
Stoic philosophy emphasised defining the self through virtues (or values) and through actions that remain within one's control.

In Eastern philosophy, Buddhism emphasises the fluidity of identity: the "self" isn't a fixed object but a process, constantly changing. This is both unsettling and liberating. It means identity can evolve with you, but can continue to evolve as you do.

Modern research recognises that our identities are important in our lives. Knowing who we are and what we stand for is important. However, research by American sociologist Dr Sheldon Stryker, third in my list of names I wish I had, confirmed that people who over-identify with a single role are more likely to experience depression and disorientation when they are too tightly bound to what they do.

The lesson here, drawn from both philosophy and academia, is that identity matters, but so does holding it lightly, with an appreciation that it has the ability to change as we do.

There are two guest interviews you should watch to provide greater insight into these subjects.

Firstly, Nick Elston shares fascinating insights on purpose and the importance of revisiting our lives to reflect on how our identity and sense of purpose have evolved.

Secondly, David Scarlett explains how he begins every day grounded in his values and beliefs, but also highlights the importance (for him) of starting every single day with a clear sense of intention.

Simply point your phone at the QR codes below to take you directly to the interviews with both David and Nick where they share these insights.

David Scarlett *Nick Elston*

Practical, Low-Cost Experiments We Can Take to Get Closer to Our Values

There's a bunch of practical low-cost, low-risk steps you can take to identify your values. I want to tell you about three...

Reflect on the Past

Think back to the three times in your life when you felt most alive, proud, or fulfilled. What were you doing? Who were you with? Why did it matter?

Often, our memories, and what we value about them the most, provide real insight about what we truly value in life.

Ask Yourself the Three Kinder Questions

Earlier in this chapter, I mentioned three questions that, I believe, offer us insight into what we truly value. These questions, popularised by the work of the brilliant George Kinder, are...

If money were no object...
Imagine you have all the money you need, now and in the future. What would you do with your life? How would you live?

If you had five to ten years left to live...
You're told you'll remain healthy but will die suddenly within five to ten years, how would you change your life?

If you had twenty-four hours left...
You learn you'll die tomorrow. What would you miss? What would you not get to do, or not get to be?

I suggest spending some time writing your answers down, thinking about these questions, and seeing what themes might emerge is a great.

Take a Quiz...
There are an amazing number of online tools that provide insights into what you value in life. One of the most insightful I've taken is the 'Values in Action' character strengths analysis. However, there are plenty of other tools which provide insight.

Many of these tools are free. These provide a 'mirror' to the way you see the world.

I found the 'Values in Action' analysis insightful, with love of learning, social intelligence and humour being my top three values. Although if anyone had heard my incredibly bad dad jokes, or experienced me making one of my terrible conversational faux pas might disagree!

After Getting Clear on Our Values, How Do We Use 'Prototyping' to Find Purpose and Evolve Our Identity?

Once you've clarified your values and translated them into small actions, you can start experimenting with identity. The idea, borrowed from design thinking, is simple...

Prototype Your life.

Don't make one giant leap into a new identity. Instead run small, reversible tests.

If you're curious about teaching, offer to run a guest lecture or mentor a younger colleague.

If community work could give you purpose, volunteer for a single project or pick a fundraising project

If you're considering more creativity in your life, join a local art class for a term.

If downshifting work, try negotiating a one-day-a-week reduction and see how it feels.

Each experiment gives you feedback. Ask yourself...

Did it energise you?

Did it drain you?

Did it feel like it brought you closer to person you want to become?

And as importantly...

Did it feel purposeful?

Remember, to maximise our wellbeing the next chapter of our lives need to have an element of purpose to balance out all of the pleasure.

The motto here is *feedback, not failure.* If something doesn't fit, that's valuable information. You've ruled something out, and this gets you a little bit closer to what you might want to actually spend your time doing.

Why Journaling Might Help You Find Purpose. Shift Your Identity and Identify Your Values

I know I'm guilty of this. I act often, but don't reflect on what I've learned often enough. In modern society, it can feel like we're moving at a hundred miles an hour. Sometimes it's worth slowing down and reflecting on what we've learned, particularly when we're navigating change and answering some of the big questions in our lives.

So another incremental action to consider as you navigate the next chapter of your life is to spend some time reflecting on what you're learning.

I'd suggest that every couple of weeks, it's worth taking thirty minutes journaling or talk with someone you trust.

Ask yourself...

- What experiments did I try this month?
- What did I learn about myself?
- Which values felt most alive?
- Where did I feel misaligned?

This turns random activity into a feedback loop. It helps you course-correct, double down on what's working, and let go of what isn't.

How to 'Wellbeing Stack' While Exploring Your New Identity and Purpose

The good news is that one of the best ways to create a new identity and explore what purpose means is to do other stuff that boosts different areas of your wellbeing. For example, if one of your values is vitality or adventure, signing up for a walking group, taking a dance class, or doing exercise could align with your values. This boosts your physical wellbeing and potentially your social wellbeing, while helping you live in line with what's important to you.

If you deeply value contribution, volunteering regularly can connect you to the community, offering a renewed sense of purpose and the opportunity to build friendships.

If you value curiosity, experimenting with a new subject can support your identity as a learner, while also sparking joy and creativity.

The good news is that many of the experiments you undertake as you navigate the next chapter of your life will naturally improve other aspects of your wellbeing, while helping you better understand your purpose and identity.

Purpose, Values, Identity and the N.E.X.T Framework

The N.E.X.T framework is a helpful way to think about identifying your values, as well as considering your identity and purpose in the next chapter of your life.

You simply start with **Navigate** by asking yourself what purpose and values look like. If you're not sure, you're probably not alone, but it's definitely worth asking yourself some thoughtful questions. Questions like...

What matters most to you?
Or...
What memories made you feel the most proud or excited?
You could even use George Kinder's three questions, an online questionnaire, or journaling to gain further insight.

Next, it's time to **Evaluate.** What feels important in your life moving forward compared to the life you're living now? How 'out of sync' do you currently feel? And what small, incremental action might help you move closer to a life aligned with your values?

Then comes **eXecute**. Choose a few low-cost experiments that help you learn more about your purpose. This might include mentoring, joining a community project, or carving out time for learning. Keep these actions small and reversible so they don't feel overwhelming.

Finally, it's time to **Track**. Regularly reflect on what you've tried by journaling or talking with someone you trust. Notice how it felt and what you learned.

Adjust as you go, knowing that your life and purpose will evolve over time. With each experiment, your identity will grow stronger yet remain flexible, moving you closer to the life you want to live in the next chapter.

Now we've started to clarify what's really important to us, the next question becomes clear.

How do we use our money to support that vision? Financial wellbeing isn't about numbers on a spreadsheet. It's about using the money we have to live the life we actually want. That's where we're heading next.

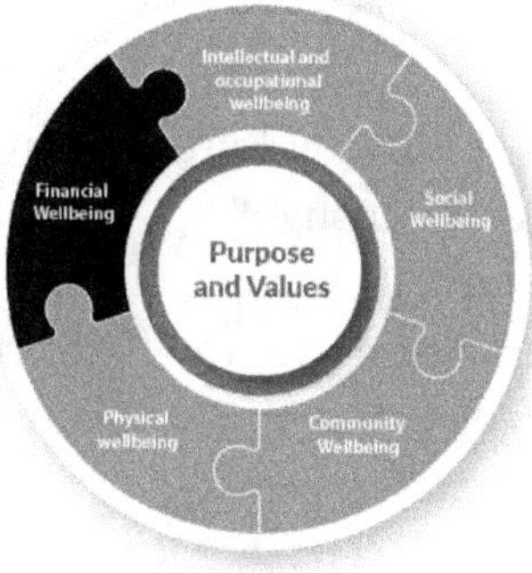

Chapter Four

Financial Wellbeing

'Money is a terrible master but an excellent servant.'
– P.T. Barnum

My all-time favourite money story was originally written as a poetry tribute from one author to another, and originally published in *The New Yorker Magazine* in 2005.

It was written by the famous author Kurt Vonnegut (the prolific writer of *Cat's Cradle* and *Slaughterhouse-Five*) to his close friend Joseph Heller (writer of the brilliantly satirical *Catch-22*) and was one of the last things Vonnegut ever published before his death in 2007.

The story describes the time when both Kurt and Joe attended the party of a billionaire and hedge fund manager.

Cheekily Kurt turns to Joe and says, 'Joe, how does it make you feel to know that our host probably made more money yesterday than your book has ever made?'

Joe simply says, 'I've got something that he'll never have.

Kurt is shocked. 'What might that be, Joe?'

Joe smiles wryly, looks at Kurt and simply exclaims, 'The knowledge that I've got enough!'

This story captures the essence of financial wellbeing. Not the biggest bank balance. Not the flashiest house. Not out-earning your neighbour, or the hedge fund billionaire who throws a party to impress others.

Financial wellbeing, at its core, is about that sense of peace that comes when you realise you've got enough resources financially to live the life you want.

And yet, for many of us, that question, 'What *is enough?*' from a financial perspective, is one of the hardest questions to answer.

Money Matters, But Not in the Way You Think

When clients first sit down with me, what I'm most curious about is what's prompted them to feel that *now* is the right time to speak to a financial planner.

Many clients come in expecting that a conversation with a financial professional will quickly turn technical on financial products and strategies.

I can't speak for every financial planner, but I don't believe talking about financial products is where the conversation should start.

At its core, money is a tool designed to help you live the life you want. Yet it's also important to recognise that each of us has a relationship with money, shaped by our experiences and the stories we tell ourselves about what it means and how it should be used.

Historically, money has simply been a way to exchange what you have for what you need. Over time, however, it's come to represent far more than that – security, freedom, success, or even stress and uncertainty.

Millennia ago, this might have been trading your grain for tools or your livestock for clothing. Today, the financial system and our relationships with money are slightly more... complicated.

It's interesting. While we're all unique, the question most people ask me is...

'Have I got enough?'

It might be framed as...

'Will I run out of money?'

Or...

'Can I afford to stop working?'

But the essence is always the same: am I safe? Will I be okay?

Financial insecurity is one of the biggest drivers of stress. Behavioural economists Sendhil Mullainathan and Eldar Shafir describe this as the *scarcity mindset.*

When money is tight, or even when we 'believe' it's tight, it narrows our focus, crowds out good decision-making, and often contributes to a consistent feeling of stress and anxiety.

Clarity is key. Even if a client is not yet financially independent, my experience has shown that simply knowing where you stand financially provides something we all want in our lives: choice.

My experience of working with financially independent clients, or with those who have financial clarity and a clear plan to achieve independence, is that this clarity creates significant opportunity.

An opportunity to plan, to live with purpose, to say no to the things that drain you, and yes to the things that give your life meaning.

Despite this, we mustn't ignore the role money plays in our lives. Research, including the work of sociologist Ruth Veenhoven and many others, shows that life satisfaction is driven far more by the quality of our relationships, a sense of purpose, and positive physical health, provided we have enough money to meet our basic needs.

The research also tells us that materialism, the pursuit of money and possessions as a means to an end, actually correlates with *lower* wellbeing.

So financial wellbeing isn't just about the treadmill of accumulating more; it's about aligning money with meaning, your values, and the life you want to live. I feel this starts with understanding where you are financially today.

The other brilliant piece of academic research worth mentioning is the study of spending money to improve our wellbeing, and the best book I've read on this subject is *Happy Money: The New Science of Smarter Spending* by Elizabeth Dunn and Michael Norton.

In this book, Dunn and Norton highlight the main ways the evidence tells us we can spend to improve our wellbeing, highlighting five specific areas where we can use our wealth to make us happier…

Spend Money on 'Experiences' over 'Stuff'

The research says that spending money on experiences over material goods increases our overall wellbeing.

Spending time actively doing something we like to do creates something really valuable for our wellbeing: memories.

The evidence suggests that while we get a small, very temporary endorphin buzz from buying more tangible goods and products, we receive a prolonged boost when we spend money on experiences. This is a triple win. We benefit from the anticipation of the experience. Then, from the actual experience. Followed by the memories accumulated from living the experience.

If it's an experience we've shared with friends or family, then we're in Brucey bonus territory, as this will enhance your wellbeing even further.

So the evidence is clear, while we might want to spend our money on both 'stuff' and 'experiences', experiences win hands down when it comes to delivering wellbeing.

Make it a Novelty

The evidence points clearly to the fact that we don't get as much happiness from something if it's not a 'treat'.

This one can feel counterintuitive. After all, if we really enjoy something, we should do more of it, right? Wrong.

One of my friends, upon retirement, told me he was going to play bucket loads of golf. He loved the game and seemed to spend every weekend at his golf club of choice.

When he stopped work, he decided to play golf even more. I remember chatting to him about five weeks after he left work. He said he was looking for something else to do.

'What happened to the non-stop golf?' I asked him.

'Well, Chris,' he told me. 'Playing all of the time made it a lot less fun.'

So if you're thinking about spending for happiness, you might want to try new things. Seek novelty and unique experiences. Spending money on the same things every day could possibly reduce the pleasure it brings, even if you love golf as much as my friend.

In the book *Happy Money*, the rules of being happy with our money are explained. Don't expect to be consistently happy doing all the things we do them all the time. In fact, it's better to spend money on things we enjoy more sparingly to get the benefit. *Happy Money* says this is 'giving yourself a treat'.

So, a holiday now and then will produce happiness, but a perpetual holiday will make us less happy.

Where golf might be fun at the weekend (as a 'treat'), it might not be fun if we do it all the time.

And...

Our imagined version of 'what happens next' is often a postcard moment: a Caribbean beach, a piña colada, nothing on the calendar. But while idyllic in short bursts, it might not float our boat if it had to be our everyday reality.

Buy Time

One of the key themes explored in *Happy Money* is using money to 'buy back' a more valuable commodity.

When thinking about my future decisions, I'm conscious that my most finite resource isn't money – it's time.

Often, my clients reach a point in their lives where they want more freedom. Understanding their financial situation helps them make the important decisions in how to spend their 'time' in the future.

This realisation inspires them to sit down with a financial planner and work out if they can afford to live the life they want.

In exploring the lives people want to live, we help them build a financial plan. In doing so, we factor in the amount necessary to cover minimum monthly bills, alongside money they'll need to do the 'fun' stuff such as travel.

However, what often gets overlooked is the need to pay for jobs you don't want to do, the ones you might not be good at. So if 'time' is arguably our most finite resource, why do we often spend it on tasks we simply don't want to do, or will take us a lot longer to do without an expert to help us?'

Happy Money has a chapter explaining why spending money on the jobs we neither love nor are good at is shown to improve our wellbeing. For example, many of us appreciate that if we're building an extension, or fitting a new bathroom, or installing a new boiler, it might be worth getting an expert in. Unless you're reading this and you are an extension builder, a bathroom fitter, or a boiler installer.

The good news is that these days there are countless ways to get someone else to take care of the jobs you'd rather not do at an affordable price.

You could employ a virtual assistant to support you with your life admin, and free more time for you to spend with friends. You could use a service like Airtasker or Fiverr.com to employ a specific expert for a specific job. You could get a travel agent to build you an ideal itinerary for your next adventure.

If you don't want to think about money every day, you could employ a financial planner. I've got one client who tells me they live a happier life knowing that, 'You, Chris, are worrying about my financial future on my behalf!'

So when you're thinking about your financial wellbeing, think about how you could spend your money efficiently and effectively to free more time doing what you love.

Pay Now, Consume Later

In today's modern, consumerist society where we're used to being instantly gratified, we tend to adhere to the idea: pay now and consume now.

In recent years, with credit becoming increasingly accessible, we've moved towards a pay later, consume now mentality. However, what if I told you that paying for a product or service now and receiving this product and service later might increase your financial wellbeing.

It seems counterintuitive, doesn't it? But there's one thing instant gratification – or delayed payment – can give you that delaying gratification does.

Anticipation. The feeling of looking forward to something.

You see, a feeling of anticipation releases dopamine in our brains, a chemical which is responsible for positive feelings.

A lot of things can produce dopamine, including some not-so-healthy habits. Gambling machines and social media produce dopamine hits. If truth be told, the betting companies and tech firms use very similar techniques to trigger these signals in the brain. The problem with the dopamine hit from a gambling machine or endlessly checking social media is that it's fleeting, requiring constant repetition just get more of the same. The benefit of 'buy later, pay now' is that the anticipation of the purchase lasts all the way until receiving the product or service.

Be Generous

One of my favourite parts of Happy *Money* was the impact that generosity to others had on our overall happiness.

When provided with a choice between taking a $10 Starbucks voucher to spend on themselves or taking a $10 Starbucks voucher and gifting it to someone else, the results were interesting. The wellbeing of the individuals who used the voucher to help someone else improved significantly more than that of the individuals who took the voucher for themselves.

Again, the evidence is clear that using our money to help others, clearly within our own dimensions of affordability, is a really good way to improve our wellbeing.

There are plenty of ways to do this, from philanthropy to sponsoring a friend, to buying someone you like a coffee, and much more.

We've evolved to be deeply social animals, and therefore it's no surprise that one of the most interesting things we can do with our money and wellbeing is to give it away! That's why Dunn calls the ability to spend money on others and improve our own wellbeing 'pro-social spending'.

The evidence in *Happy Money* is clear...

Spending money on other people makes us happy too, and there are a bunch of ways you can do this...

- You can buy a friend a gift.
- You could treat your wife, your kids or a friend to lunch.
- Less obviously, and taking examples from my own life, you could sponsor a local kids' football team, making sure the kids are kept in shirts and shorts for the next season.
- You could support and pay for a financial education program at an educational institution you care about.
- You could buy a guy living on the street a pork pie.

So we've looked at what the research says about knowing where we stand financially, having a healthy relationship with money, and understanding how spending can improve our wellbeing. However, the conversations we have in the modern world about money aren't anything new. For millennia, philosophers have explored our relationship with money and highlighted insights worth sharing, often validating up-to-date research.

Philosophical Lenses on Money

Aristotle wrote about money as a means, not an end. Wealth, he argued, is only valuable insofar as it helps us live a flourishing life. If money is pursued for its own sake, it distorts our purpose.

This validates so much of the research and shows that relationships are way more important than our financial situation in our overall wellbeing, as long as we understand our definition of 'enough'.

The Stoics taught us to distinguish between what we can and cannot control. When it comes to money, I try to incorporate this into my own life and that of my clients.

For example, we can control the necessary strategy to achieve our financial goals. After covering our basic needs, we can decide how much to save and how much to spend. And if we feel we need support, we can choose to get help with our financial affairs.

The Stoics would also argue that we can control our emotions. I would argue that this means we can control our responses to our financial ups and downs. But there are definitely things you can't control, and the Stoics would suggest these things are not worth worrying about. You can't control investment markets or political policies. You can't control what other people think, or the events which impact our lives.

I think the Stoics were right. In my personal experience, the clients who have a great relationship with money, financial security and can spend happily also have a healthy perspective on what they can control and what they can't.

I also think there's a bucket load of truth in the quote from renowned Stoic Epictetus, who said, 'Wealth consists not in having great possessions... but in having few wants.'

Guest Insights

We've interviewed some brilliant people for *What Happens Next* about the importance of our relationships with money and financial wellbeing in our lives. I am going to start with Chris Budd and Catherine Morgan...

When I spoke with Chris Budd, founder of the Institute for Financial Wellbeing, what struck me was his simple but powerful message: financial wellbeing is not about how much money you accumulate, it's about how you use it to create happiness.

Chris argued that too many of us fall into the trap of focusing on wealth as a scorecard, rather than a tool. He highlighted research showing that once our basic needs are covered, more money doesn't necessarily make us happier. Instead, the real benefits come when we consciously link money to the things that matter most to us – relationships, experiences, contribution, and freedom of time.

Chris described financial wellbeing as the intersection between money and meaning. His practical advice was to spend deliberately: 'If you're thinking about your financial wellbeing, work out what makes you happy and spend money on that.'

This aligns perfectly with the work of Dunn and Norton in *Happy Money* and reinforces the idea that defining 'enough' is deeply personal. Chris' insight was a timely reminder that financial wellbeing is not about chasing the next shiny thing, but about creating alignment between our finances and the lives we want to live.

My conversation with Catherine Morgan centred on the stories we tell ourselves about money – and how those stories can either support or sabotage our wellbeing. Catherine, a financial coach, explained that many of us carry inherited beliefs, or 'money stories' from childhood. For some, it's a story of scarcity: there's never enough, and there never will be. For others, it's a story of shame: money is bad, or people with money are greedy.

These unconscious narratives shape how we behave with money as adults, sometimes helping us but often holding us back.

Catherine's work is about helping people notice these stories, understand where they come from, and decide whether they still serve them.

What I found particularly powerful was her emphasis on rewriting those stories. By choosing new narratives, ones grounded in agency, gratitude, and possibility, we can change not just our financial habits, but our overall sense of wellbeing.

Catherine reminded me that two people can have the same bank balance but feel completely different about their financial security, depending on the story they tell themselves. Her message was clear: financial wellbeing is as much about mindset and meaning as it is about money itself.

To watch these interviews now, simply point your phone at the QR codes, and it'll take you directly to the interview.

Chris Budd

Catherine Morgan

Practical, Low-Cost Experiments to Improve Your Financial Wellbeing

You don't need to overhaul your entire financial life overnight. In fact, small experiments often create the biggest shifts. Here are a few you might want to try...

Spend some time getting closer to your own personal definition of 'enough' financially.

I'd suggest the starting point for this isn't a spreadsheet, but simply a question we've talked about in this book before: 'If you knew you'd always have enough money, how would you spend your time?'

It's unlikely to be a single answer, and chances are the ways you'd like to spend your time on will be a relatively long list.

For most people, how they'd spend their time with unlimited money includes a decent chunk of travel, helping the people you love financially and having novel experiences, which have always been on the 'someday' list. However, for many people, a lot of the things on this list are simple.

Typically, for many people, the list includes the time and space for a daily walk, the opportunity to take the young people in your life to the park, and simply spending more time with people you love and like.

So the big question to then ask is...

If the things you want to do don't cost much, what's the small next step you can take to do more of that now?

For everything else, it might be the right time to think about how much these things cost.

Below is a QR code that will take you to a budget planner. This will help you think about how much you need to spend to live your 'enough'.

Once you've understood how much you need to live the life you want, you've got a bunch of options...

One option is to work with a high-quality financial planner who will help you discover if you've got a gap or not.

There are real advantages to this. A good planner will take the complexity off your shoulders, translate jargon into clarity, and create a long-term plan that helps you live with confidence.

They can run the numbers, stress test your finances against different scenarios (market downturns, unexpected expenses, longer life expectancy), and, crucially, hold you accountable to the plan when life throws curveballs.

I'd suggest that for my clients, the peace of mind of knowing someone else is providing clarity, helping them make important decisions and taking all the data – alongside my knowledge and a pinch of technological tools – and turning it into a plan which allows them to have clarity to live the life they want, is super valuable.

However, financial planning isn't for everyone.

There are costs involved, and not every planner brings the same mix of technical skill and empathy. Some people prefer to stay hands-on and enjoy the sense of control that comes from managing their own plan. For others, particularly if money conversations trigger anxiety, the act of sitting down with a planner might feel intimidating at first.

So if doing this with someone like me really fills you with dread, I would suggest you use the '4% rule'. Basically, if you've got a pot of invested money, you withdraw 4% of your invested assets each year, factoring in inflation.

The 4% rule is a quick and simple calculation and is only designed to provide you with a ballpark number in relation to how much wealth might be enough.

The challenge is that it ignores so many factors, including tax rules, market changes, living longer, and the fact that most people don't have a fixed spending pattern from their mid-50s until they die.

There's no one-size-fits-all approach to working out your 'enough', but starting with how you'd like to spend your time, and working out how much that might cost on a regular basis is, I'd suggest, step one.

Understand What Spending Gives You Joy

For one week, track not only what you spend, but also how each purchase makes you feel.

I'd suggest you keep it simple:

Every time you spend a bit of money, simply record the item, the cost, and rate the joy it brought on a scale of 1 to 10. As I write this, there's even an app (Daylio) that allows you to link your mood at the time with your activity.

The idea here is to notice surprising patterns. That £3 coffee with a friend might score higher than the £300 gadget you used once. A train ticket to visit family might feel far more satisfying than the dinner out you barely remember.

The benefit of this exercise is twofold. First, it highlights 'leaky' spending, those small, habitual purchases that add little to your wellbeing.

Second, it reveals where even modest amounts of money can bring disproportionate joy. You may discover that experiences, connections, or novelty deliver more lasting happiness than the latest upgrade.

The goal isn't to shame yourself for spending, but to spot where your money genuinely aligns with your values. Over time, you can redirect funds away from low-joy spending and towards what truly matters. Many people find that this exercise shifts their mindset from 'budgeting as restriction' to 'spending as choice', which is a far more empowering frame.

For one week, track not only what you spend, but also how each purchase makes you feel. Keep it simple: jot down the item, the cost, and rate the joy it brings on a scale of 1–10. You may notice surprising patterns. That £3 coffee with a friend might score higher than the £300 gadget you used once. A train ticket to visit family might feel far more satisfying than the dinner out you barely remember.

Write a Letter to 86 ½ -Year-Old You

Set aside twenty minutes to imagine yourself aged 86½. Now, write a letter from that future self, back to the person you are today.

What would they thank you for doing financially? Perhaps saving consistently, saying yes to experiences, or spending time with loved ones instead of chasing more.

Just as importantly, what would they urge you to stop worrying about? The sleepless nights over market dips, or the guilt of spending money on things that brought joy?

This exercise is designed to provide perspective. Often, we're so caught up in today's pressures that we lose sight of what will matter decades from now. The letter helps you reframe decisions through the lens of long-term meaning rather than short-term anxiety. It also surfaces the values that underpin your definition of 'enough'.

Wellbeing Stacking: The Practical Activities You Can Do to Improve Your Financial Wellbeing and Other Areas of Wellbeing in Your Life

Basically, improving your financial wellbeing can improve your wellbeing in many aspects of your life.

After all, if you've ever turned down a social occasion or adventure holiday because you *felt* you 'couldn't afford it', when in reality you simply weren't clear whether you could afford it or not, then your social wellbeing and physical wellbeing might have been negatively impacted.

However, there are also a bunch of low-cost, experimental and practical things you can do to improve both your financial wellbeing.

Learn More About Money

One of the simplest ways to improve your financial wellbeing is to build your financial literacy a little at a time. Learning doesn't need to mean studying economics or poring over investment charts.

It can be as simple as reading a personal finance book from the library, listening to a podcast on the school run, or watching a trusted YouTube channel that explains concepts in plain English.

Financial wellbeing improves because you gain financial

clarity and confidence. Learning new skills then boosts intellectual wellbeing, providing you with a potential double win.

Volunteering

Volunteering doesn't just help others. It can provide a sense of purpose and meaning in our lives, can enhance our community wellbeing, expand our social network (improving our social wellbeing), but it can also have an interesting impact on our financial wellbeing.

Helping others assists our financial wellbeing often by increasing our levels of gratitude. A recent study by Dali Hayward and Rona Hart found that a person's tendency to be thankful is simply their ability to be grateful and positively contributes to lowering their financial stress.

Who'd have thunk it! Helping others is good for our financial wellbeing too.

Giving to Others

We already know from the brilliant work in *Happy Money* that we improve our financial wellbeing by helping others.

However, giving gifts can also improve our social wellbeing (think about the positive emotions you felt the last time you gave or received a gift).

But not all gifts are given to people we know. You can positively enhance your community wellbeing and your financial wellbeing by gifting money or resources to causes you believe in, too.

Financial Wellbeing and the N.E.X.T Framework

The N.E.X.T framework is also a really useful way to think about your financial wellbeing, and whether money is supporting the life you want to live. It doesn't need to be complicated – it's simply a way of asking good questions and taking small, practical steps.

You start with **Navigate**. This is about clarifying where you want to go. What does financial wellbeing look like for you? What experiences, freedoms, or opportunities matter most?

A useful starting question we've touched on before is: *'If you knew you'd always have enough money, how would you spend your time?'*

For some people, it's travel, for others it's helping children or grandchildren, for others still it's simply more space for rest and connection. Define the direction of travel first, which means thinking about your version of 'enough.'

Next, it's time to **Evaluate.** Here, you get clear on where you are right now. What money comes in each month? What goes out? What do you own and what do you owe? You don't need a perfect spreadsheet, just a simple map of your current financial position.

Ask yourself: *What do I already know about my money? What feels uncertain or confusing?* Even this act of noticing often reduces anxiety.

Then it's **eXecute**. Choose a couple of low-cost experiments that move you closer to your version of financial wellbeing. This might include giving to others or improving your own money knowledge.

Finally, it's time to **Track**. It's time to reflect regularly on what you've tried and what you've learned.

Did the spending diary you completed reveal surprising patterns? Did saving a small amount each week make you feel lighter?

You could jot these reflections in a journal or talk them through with a friend or partner. Over time, these small check-ins build clarity and confidence, and you'll find your financial wellbeing growing stronger and more stable with every experiment.

In this chapter, we've explored why financial wellbeing is way deeper than simply the numbers. It's about the peace that comes from knowing you've got enough, the clarity of money with meaning, and the freedom to make choices that fit your values. I hope that regardless of the stories you tell yourself about money and whether you're super confident or very nervous financially, the tips shared in this chapter allow you to incrementally improve your overall financial wellbeing.

However, money is only part of the picture, and there's a topic we now need to discuss, which many would suggest underpins other aspects of wellbeing. It's our physical wellbeing and in the next chapter, let's explore how we can incrementally improve in this area of our lives...

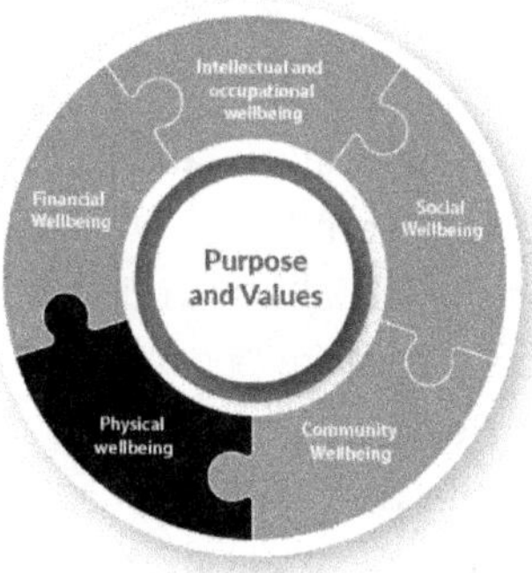

Chapter Five

Physical Wellbeing

'Take care of your body. It's the only place you have to live.'
– Jim Rohn

He'd spent years in a job which was intellectually challenging but ultimately draining. Every week felt the same. Long hours, high stress levels, late-night emails and dinner on the go.

By the time we'd met with Steve, who was in his early sixties, he already had a few health warning signs. A recent medical had shown high cholesterol, and blood pressure, his joints were aching, and he was waking up after a restless night's sleep already tired.

Initially, he'd taken these signals simply as a sign of getting older. However, he knew the truth. He'd neglected his health and had to make a positive change for the better.

Our initial conversations started when we talked about business. Then, we talked about money and the concept of financial independence. In the end, as our relationship continued to grow, we talked about the important stuff. Friendship. Happiness. Family.

We also talked about health and this gentleman's realisation that he should probably make a positive change.

The problem? He hated gyms. He didn't play sports. He felt running wasn't for him.

So his health improvement didn't start with a personal trainer, a diet of leaves and broccoli, or sweating half of your body weight on a spin bike.

It started with his dog.

One Autumn Monday morning, after Steve had spent the weekend dropping his son off at university, dragged himself out of bed. That's when he realised, the dog needed walking and his son wasn't there to do it anymore.

This started a new habit. A habit which he told me later had a massive positive impact on each area of his life.

Every morning, before emails, before breakfast, before the rest of life had a chance to grab him by the collar, he went for a walk in the forest with the dog.

At first, it was purely pragmatic. The dog needed walking. But something happened. That simple act of lacing up his shoes and heading into the path between the trees set the tone for his entire day. The walk gave him space to breathe, to think, to simply exist without a to-do list in front of him. Slowly, other things shifted too.

Steve began to realise that he could make additional simple changes to his physical wellbeing. These would not only make him feel better, but also help him think more clearly. He started to make incrementally positive choices health-wise too. Better food choices, better sleep habits and reducing the amount of booze he consumed.

Steve still loved a drink or two, and the odd fry-up, but realised that he was now more conscious of the choices he made.

Steve told me later that he also realised something else. He always told himself he didn't have the time to be more physically healthy. He'd realised that, like anything important in our lives, we had to make time and build habits in our lives which ensure we keep consistent.

That's the thing about physical wellbeing. It rarely starts with a grand gesture or some glossy health plan. Often, it begins with something embarrassingly simple. Like walking the dog.

Why Physical Wellbeing Matters

When my client started walking his dog each morning, he wasn't thinking about blood pressure, cholesterol, or longevity. He just wanted to feel a little less rubbish. But science is clear: even small shifts in how we move, rest, and fuel ourselves have a huge impact.

The World Health Organisation suggests that just one hundred and fifty minutes of moderate movement a week – that's about twenty minutes a day – lowers your risk of heart disease, diabetes, and depression. Studies also show that light daily exercise, like a brisk walk, can reduce blood pressure, improve sleep quality, and even sharpen memory and concentration.

Sleep, too, is often underrated. Dr Matthew Walker, author of *Why We Sleep*, has shown how even one week of sleeping less than six hours a night can impair immunity, increase stress hormones, and reduce your ability to learn new information. It's no wonder Dr Neil Stanley told us in his interview featured in this book that sleep is the single most effective performance-enhancing habit you can adopt.

Nutrition is another layer. Research from Harvard's School of Public Health highlights how diets rich in whole foods – vegetables, fruit, legumes, whole grains –reduce chronic disease risk, while high sugar and processed food diets contribute to inflammation and low energy. But again, it's not about perfection. It's about balance and the habits you can actually sustain.

The early indicators of change are often subtle but powerful: slightly lower blood pressure, a steadier resting heart rate, better sleep, fewer afternoon slumps, less stiffness when you wake. These are the small green shoots that show your body is responding, often within weeks of small adjustments.

Perhaps most importantly, physical wellbeing is a force multiplier. Better energy and sleep improve decision-making (including financial ones), mood stability improves relationships, and improved mobility means you can join in more fully with the people and activities you love.

This chapter isn't about chasing six-packs or training for ultra-marathons. It's about ensuring you've got the energy and vitality to do the things you've always wanted to do in a period of your life where you've probably hit a bit of a sweet spot.

If we think about the way that our physical health, financial health and amount of available time changes over the years, many of us hit a bit of a sweet spot in our fifties and sixties.

When we're a lot younger, many of us have high levels of physical health, plenty of time, but are financially normally at the starting line.

Then, often kids come along, and we become more financially stable, but on the flipside, life becomes busier than ever. So we're in a better financial situation, still in pretty good physical health, but often 'time' poor.

Then something slowly changes. We've continued to build our financial resources, potentially to a point where we get a lot more control over how we spend our time, and our health might also be pretty good too.

This means we've got the time, the money, the energy and vitality to live the life we want.

However, here's the kicker. Often the thing as we hit out fifties, sixties, seventies and eighties, is the something that potentially stop us living the life we want: a decline in our physical health.

That's why focusing on maintaining great habits, designed to maintain positive physical health, is so important in this period of our lives.

The Stoics talked about how exercise a decent amount. Seneca, when famously writing about the importance of physical challenge to improve our mental state, said, 'We treat the body rigorously, so that it may not be disobedient to the mind.'

For the Stoics, exercise was away to prepare for adversity and a way to help us become a little more resilient.

However, the Stoics were also massive fans of maintaining a 'golden mean', which is all about exercising enough to build strength and resilience but also living well.

They were also about building in daily habits. These include modest, consistent activity like walking or strength training to live a balanced life. In many ways, they were millennia ahead of what we know from the science on health. Consistency beats intensity virtually every time.

It also means that we don't need to feel too guilty when we enjoy a big Sunday roast, a glass of wine and a chocolate flake in our ice cream. If the Stoics were right and balance was key, we should be able to do a bit of what we enjoy as part of the mix.

Buddhist thought also emphasises awareness of the body. The practice of mindful walking, for example, is about noticing each step, each breath reminding us that wellbeing can be cultivated in the simplest daily movements.

I often find it interesting when you consider the common message when exploring both eastern and western philosophy, and when it comes to physical wellbeing the message is clear.

Physical wellbeing isn't about how you look or how many marathons you run. It's about the right balance for you, and ensuring that you're able to live a long, happy and healthy life.

If philosophy gives us some of the theories, the 'blue zones' research by Dan Buettner's into the world's longest-living communities, from Okinawa in Japan to Ikaria in Greece, shows that longevity and vitality are rarely the result of gym memberships or restrictive diets. Instead, they flow from deeply embedded cultural habits.

Across the blue zones, people move naturally as part of daily life. They tend their gardens, they walk to visit neighbours (often in hilly terrains) and they often continue working with their hands.

The blue zone's meals are mostly simple, mostly plant-based, and enjoyed socially. Crucially, physical wellbeing is not a separate 'activity' bolted onto life, it's woven into how they live their lives.

These places teach us that physical wellbeing thrives when it is simple, social, and sustainable. Steve's story echoes this truth. He didn't overhaul his life overnight.

He started walking the dog. And from that one small, sustainable act, ripples spread into his sleep, nutrition, mood, and mindset.

Physical Wellbeing Guest Insights from What Happens Next

Maintaining positive physical health is a theme that comes up with our guest's time and time again, and we've been fortunate enough to have some amazing experts share their insights.

Sleep expert Dr Neil Stanley told me during our interview, 'Sleep is the single most effective performance-enhancing habit we know.' He explained that sleep is not passive downtime but active maintenance for the brain and body. During deep sleep, memories are consolidated, toxins are cleared from the brain, and the immune system resets.

If the next chapter of your life looks anything like mine, it'll demand energy, creativity, and resilience. Sleep is the foundation that enables all three. And yet, like Steve, many people only confront their sleep when health warning signs show up. As Neil reminded us, you shouldn't wait for a crisis before you take care of your body.

When it comes to nutrition, Georgia, a nutritionist I spoke with, put it bluntly: 'A diet you can't stick to isn't a diet – it's a punishment.' Georgia emphasised that nutrition is about building habits that fit into your real life, not chasing extremes.

This echoes what we see in research from Harvard's School of Public Health: long-term wellbeing comes from diets rich in whole foods, legumes, vegetables, and whole grains, not short-term fad restrictions. But the best diet is always the one you can maintain.

Georgia also reminded me that food is culture, not just calories. In blue zone regions like Okinawa or Sardinia, meals are rarely eaten alone or in front of a screen. They are social rituals, often simple, often plant-based, but always connected to community. Eating is not just fuel, it's fellowship. That social layer may be just as important to wellbeing as the nutrients on the plate.

Exercise, too, was reframed by several of our guests. Jamie Harrison, who founded the *Consistency Club*, spoke about how easy it is to fall into 'all or nothing' thinking when it comes to exercise. His message was clear. Stop chasing perfection, and instead build small, consistent habits that you can build on.

You can find the interviews with Dr Neil Stanley, Georgia Farrar and Jamie Harrison here. Simple click the QR codes below...

Dr Neil Stanley | *Georgia Farrar* | *Jamie Harrison*

Practical Low-cost Experiments to Improve Your Physical Wellbeing

You don't need to become a marathon runner, hire a personal trainer, or survive on kale smoothies to make progress with your physical wellbeing.

In fact, the biggest improvements usually come from small, low-cost experiments you can try today. Here's a few to kick you off...

Start With the 'Twenty-Minute Walk' Rule

Most of us tell ourselves we don't have time to exercise. But what Steve discovered (and what many of our guests have said) is that the simplest movement is often the most effective.

So here's the experiment: commit to twenty minutes of

walking a day. That could be with your dog, with your partner, or on your own while listening to music or a podcast. The key is consistency. Don't worry about pace or distance. Simply work to build the habit.

Many people find that twenty minutes turns into thirty or forty without noticing. The benefit is not only in the exercise itself, but also in the mental space it creates to think, breathe, and reset before the day grabs hold of you.

Try a Digital Sunset

If sleep is the master habit, then how we prepare for it matters. For three nights this week, switch off screens an hour before bed. That means no TV, no phone, no laptop.

Use the time instead to read, stretch, journal, or simply wind down. Notice how it changes the quality of your sleep, not just the number of hours. Many people report deeper, more refreshing rest after even a few nights of this experiment.

Make One Swap a Day

Rather than overhauling your diet, try one small food swap each day. Replace crisps with fruit, fizzy drinks with water, or your fry-up with eggs and spinach.

The idea isn't to become 'perfect' but to gently nudge your choices. This experiment helps you spot the swaps that feel easy and sustainable, not forced.

Begin with a Standing Start

How you begin your morning often sets the tone for the whole day. Before emails, news, or social media, take two minutes to stretch. Roll your shoulders, reach for the ceiling, touch your toes.

It's a simple way to signal to yourself that movement matters. It also wakes up your body before you dive into the mental demands of the day.

Set Yourself a Bedtime

I don't know about you, but the area of physical wellbeing I've personally struggled with the most over the years is consistent sleep habits.

Exercise I'm normally pretty consistent with and my nutrition, while I'm still keen on the odd Cadbury's cream egg, has definitely improved over the last few years.

Good sleep habits have been really elusive, but I've recently started to improve these habits by simply setting a bedtime on my phone.

At that time an alarm goes off and my phone screen goes grey, which tells me it's time to sleep. This simple 'nudge' in the direction of a more positive sleep habit doesn't work every time, but helps remind me what I need to improve.

I often think that, as an adult, setting my own bedtime feels like a childlike thing to do. Surely if I'm an adult, I definitely don't need to do that!

However, my recent experience tells me that positive habits at the end of the day mean that I have loads more vitality the following day and more energy in my life.

How to 'Wellbeing Stack' When Improving Your Physical Wellbeing

The good news is that when it comes to improving our physical wellbeing there's so many simple ways we can do this, particularly while exercising and eating better.

Walking With a Friend

A brisk walk ticks off your daily movement quota, lowers stress, and keeps your joints moving. But when you invite a friend along, it also strengthens your social ties.

So, what looks like 'just a walk' is an investment in both your physical and social wellbeing.

Cooking With Your Family

I always saw cooking as a 'solo sport' until a few weeks ago I was talking with a friend of mine who cooks with his family.

He told me that as a family they're not only more conscious of what they eat but it becomes a daily communal event which provides an opportunity to talk and spend time with each other, enhancing both your social and physical wellbeing at the same time.

Exercise in Your Community – The GoodGym Concept

From padel, to slinging my limbs about in a kickboxing class to jumping up and down at a park-based boot camp, I've always found it easier to exercise with others.

Whether it's a walking club, a yoga class at the local hall, or a weekly five-a-side football game, community exercise blends movement with social connection. It often comes with accountability (someone notices if you're not there), and that makes habits stick.

However, I reckon the best modern example of combining the advantages of both fitness and community is UK based Goodgym.

GoodGym turns ordinary workouts into acts of service. Instead of lifting weights in a gym, members run to visit isolated older people, deliver groceries, or help community projects. The idea is simple but powerful. Use the energy you'd normally spend on exercise to do good in your local area.

For participants, the benefits stack up. You get the cardiovascular workout from running or cycling, the mental wellbeing boost of volunteering, and the social connection of being part of a group. For the community, it means extra hands for projects that matter and human connection for people who might otherwise feel forgotten.

Applying the N.E.X.T model to Physical Wellbeing

The N.E.X.T framework is also a really useful way to think about your physical wellbeing and whether your body is supporting the life you want to live.

You start with **Navigate**. This means clarifying where you want to go. What does physical wellbeing look like for you? Is it having the energy to travel? or playing football with grandkids without gasping for breath?

Is it more about feeling rested enough to think clearly? Or being able to do the tip run without putting your back out?

Next, it's time to **Evaluate**.

Where are you now, honestly? How much daily movement are you getting? How many hours of sleep do you typically have? What about your nutrition? Are you fuelling your body well, or mostly grabbing what's convenient? You might choose to use fitness trackers to provide the insight however often it starts with asking yourself some open and honest questions about how your exercise, nutrition and sleep habits are today.

Then comes **eXecute**. This is about taking action in small, sustainable ways. Choose one or two low-cost experiments you can try this week.

For Steve, it was walking the dog before breakfast.

For you, you might want to follow the 'top tip' from our brilliant what happens next guest and expert nutritionist Georgia Farrar. Simply swap one food that might not be as good for you with something more healthy on a regular basis.

The key is not to chase perfection, but to start where you are with something you can realistically repeat.

Finally, it's time to **Track**. Reflect on what's working and what isn't. Did a twenty-minute walking habit lift your energy or improve your mood? Did turning off your screens an hour before bed help you wake up more refreshed?

Recording the progress you're making, either in a journal or using your phone, can both motivate but also make you more conscious of the health decisions you make.

For many physical wellbeing is the foundation. It gives us the energy, clarity, and resilience to live the lives we want.

But as I've discovered in countless conversations in researching this book, my experience of working with clients, physical health alone isn't enough.

As humans we are wired for connection and not getting this connection can have huge detrimental effects on our physical health (more on this in the next chapter).

The longest-lived people in the blue zones don't just move naturally and eat well. They also belong to strong social networks where friendships, family bonds, and community ties run deep.

The truth is you can be as physically health as you want but there's a crucial piece we need to make sure we discuss which many scientists argue is the most important contributor to our overall wellbeing.

Which is why we need to talk about the next piece of the puzzle when navigating the next chapter of our lives, Social Wellbeing.

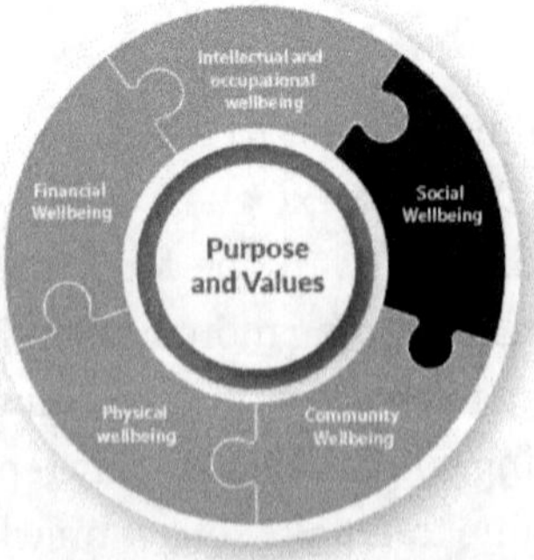

Chapter Six

Social Wellbeing

'The quality of our relationships determines the quality of our lives.' – Esther Perel

If you looked at my life ten years ago, you'd have assumed it was one of relative success.

A man in his late thirties with his own business, which after a scary and rocky start, was growing steadily. An amazing wife and two brilliant daughters.

However, the reality was a little different. Financially, I had stability. I had a family who loved me. I had pretty good health, although with hindsight I'm not sure my then obsession with Cadbury's cream eggs was helping me that much.

Despite this, one area of my life was lacking. I didn't spend much time with my friends.

I also knew the reason why. In a desire to get my business to a point where it felt secure, I'd neglected the relationships I'd built with my friends.

I still had friends, but as life had become increasingly busy because of work and family, I'd only see them a handful of times a year.

The interesting thing is I didn't feel particularly lonely. I was often surrounded by people at work and at home. However, I started to realise that, despite this, I rarely had a group of mates with whom I could just talk things through.

At the same time, my eldest daughter Charlotte was turning thirteen and I was worried. I'd thought I'd done a 'fairly' decent job as Dad, but I was also worried that I wasn't equipped to navigate the teenage years.

In a desire to connect with Charlotte and maintain a relationship, I decided that it'd be a great idea to host a podcast together. So, through interviews with people doing brilliantly kind things in the world, I'd learn to be a kinder human and (hopefully) a better dad!

It was during one of these interviews, where we interviewed a bloke called Jason, my perspective on friendships started to change.

You see, Jason and I were similar in many ways. Busy at work, busy at home and had neglected proper social connection.

Jason, to help others and give something back, had volunteered for Age UK's befriending service. This is a service designed to help prevent loneliness in older people, where Age UK connect someone typically younger (in their thirties or forties) with someone a bit older (someone in their late seventies or eighties). Typically, it worked like this...

Every week Jason used to phone a lady called Dellis, who was a Liverpudlian born and bred. Dellis was in her eighties and had lived a life. They shared a love of music with Dellis regaling Jason with the experience of seeing The Beatles in the Cavern Club before they'd become 'big'.

Dellis' husband had passed away a few years previously, and her family, while seeing her every now and again, had moved away. Dellis loved to chat, as Jason found out, but during their relationship Jason found something interesting happening.

At first, Jason admits, he saw it as a one-way street.

He was offering companionship to someone who was lonely and this meant that the first calls were polite, slightly awkward, with both of them figuring out what to say. But then something shifted. A story about music sparked a shared memory. A laugh about the weather became a running joke. Slowly, the formality dissolved and what was meant to be 'help' became a genuine friendship.

The 'Help' reference wasn't an intentional Beatles' pun by the way. Sometimes they happen, sometimes they don't... like today, I'm full of Beatles' puns, but I couldn't think of any 'Yesterday'.

Don't worry... I'll get my coat.

In the meantime, let's get on with the story...

Jason told me later, 'I thought I was volunteering. But I was just making a friend. Dellis is my mate now.'

Over time, their conversations became a highlight of his week. He found himself looking forward to their chats, curious about her stories, grateful for her perspective. Dellis, in turn, said the calls made her feel less invisible, less cut off from the world.

What started as charity became reciprocity. Jason gave his time, and in return received connection, wisdom, and the rare gift of seeing life through someone else's eyes.

I found myself thinking a lot about Jason's story, what it could teach me about friendship, and how I could use the lessons Jason learned from Dellis and vice versa.

I think there are two elements to my lesson. Firstly, consistency matters. Jason and Dellis didn't chat once every few months, or during religious holidays. They had a ritual of a weekly phone call, which deepened their relationship and increased their social bonds over time.

Secondly, Jason was happier because of this relationship and Dellis was too. Being around and regularly connected to people we love and like is really important to our health and wellbeing.

That's when I met my mate, Mike, and learned a lot from him about friendship.

You see, Mike is brilliant at one thing. *Trying* to be social.

You see, what Mike does brilliantly is try. He's brilliant at setting dates and getting people together. He's brilliant at carving out the time to check in with people. He is brilliant at taking the time to organise opportunities to get people together. He's simply brilliant at 'making an effort' to engage people socially, and seems to intrinsically understand that it takes a bit of work.

My brilliant wife, Cassie, is the same. She ensures that she reaches out, sets dates, makes plans, suggests ideas, and makes a massive effort to reach out to people on a regular basis.

However, many of us (including me) have done quite the opposite. If you don't reach out to a friend, life gets busy and we find ourselves not speaking, or messaging someone for weeks, then months, and potentially years.

Then, it becomes more and more awkward. Neither of you intended to erode the friendship. Life simply gets in the way.

People like Mike and Cassie don't do that. They invest time to regularly check in.

They appreciate we're all busy, but prioritise time in their days to make sure us less than proactive people (I could have and probably should have used the phrase lazy sods there!) need a nudge to be a bit better socially.

So what can we do to improve our social wellbeing? The first step is simple...

I reckon we should all 'be more Mike' or 'be more Cassie'. Actually, that's good. Maybe I should get that printed on a t-shirt!

We should make the effort to send that WhatsApp message. To post in the WhatsApp group. To arrange dates and set up times to get together. We should make more calls. We should carve out time to enjoy each other's company.

Why? Because as we'll talk about in this chapter. The evidence is clear. Our social wellbeing is fundamentally important to our overall wellbeing.

This seems like a perfect opportunity to take a look at the evidence...

What the Longest Study on Happiness Taught Us About Friendship

If you'd asked most people what makes a good life, they'd probably say something about money, career success, health or a combination of these three. Those answers make perfect sense as they're the values society often implicitly and explicitly suggests are important to aim for.

Now don't get me wrong. Health, wealth and work are component points of a successful life, and it's the reasons we talk about all of these things in this book.

However, one of the things which is constantly and consistently ignored in the societal definition of success is the importance of our relationships, and the fact that great social connections have an oversized impact to our wellbeing.

Friendships and pigs in blankets, and research going back over eighty years clearly shows the importance of the first element. The latter might just be me.

You see as far back as 1938, a group of researchers at Harvard University set out to answer one of life's biggest questions. *What really makes us flourish?*

They followed two groups of young men. One group of Harvard sophomores, including, famously, a young John F. Kennedy and another group of boys from the poorer neighbourhoods of Boston. The idea was to track their entire lives and see what truly mattered when it came to happiness for someone throughout their life.

They didn't just send a survey once and call it a day. They met them regularly, they took blood samples, reviewed medical notes, interviewed their partners and children, and they kept doing that for over eighty years.

It's now known as the Harvard Study of Adult Development, although it's often called the Harvard Study of Happiness. It's still being conducted today, often with the children and grandchildren of the original participants, and is, by a long stretch, the longest study into wellbeing ever conducted.

The Harvard Study of Adult Development is a longitudinal study. This means that it follows and continues to follow the same people over time. This is really important.

You see, most research gives you a snapshot, and there's a real problem with working out what supports our wellbeing when we take snapshots. We don't get a clear picture. We all go through periods of our lives that are more challenging than others, and where we might have trouble. A snapshot in our wellbeing, therefore, carries the risk of providing information that could be misleading or skewed by the circumstances of a particular moment in an individual's life.

A longer-term perspective more likely to account for the ups and downs and highs and lows. By looking at lifetime wellbeing, we can uncover some fascinating insights about what truly constitutes a life well lived.

So what did the researchers find after eighty-plus years of data, analysis, and a small mountain of questionnaires?

Put simply,

"The quality of our relationships determines the quality of our lives"

Of course, there are many factors that impact our lives, but having strong, meaningful social connections plays a crucial role in how our lives turn out.

It almost sounds too simple, doesn't it? It's not fame or fortune that brings satisfaction. It's not how many followers you've got on Instagram, or connections on Facebook. It all comes down to high-quality social connections.

Also, the evidence from both the Harvard study and other research on the impact of positive wellbeing continues to pile up.

In the study, the people who were most satisfied in their relationships at age fifty were the healthiest at age eighty.

An independent study looked at everything from cholesterol levels to brain scans, and researchers found that the same continuous truth kept showing up: strong, supportive social connections protect our bodies and our minds.

People who were lonely or disconnected had higher levels of stress hormones, weaker immune systems, and sharper declines in memory as they aged. Those surrounded by friends, family, or even just a sense of belonging, lived longer and reported more joy.

All the evidence also points to the fact that, put bluntly, loneliness has a massive negative impact on our health.

The U.S. Surgeon General has compared the health impact of chronic loneliness to smoking fifteen cigarettes a day. It makes me wonder if loneliness has such a detrimental impact on our health, why most of us are far more likely to worry about giving up smoking than about keeping our friendships alive.

What I love about the Harvard study is that it doesn't just tell us why connection matters, it shows us how it works.

Many of the happiest people they tracked didn't have perfect lives. They had ups and downs, divorces, illnesses, and financial problems. But they had someone they could rely on when things got rough. Their relationships acted as a buffer against stress. Friendships helped a bit like an emotional immune system.

There's something deeply reassuring about that, isn't there? You don't have to have everything in life sorted. You just need the right people around you to cheer you on when things goes right, but also be there for you when things don't.

So when the Harvard study concluded that 'the quality of our relationships determines the quality of our lives', they were, in a sense, rediscovering what philosophers have been saying for more than two thousand years.

Long before wellness trackers and brain scans, the great thinkers were trying to understand what makes life meaningful, and almost all of them ended up circling back to one idea: we are, at our core, social creatures.

Aristotle called friendship one of the highest virtues, ranking it just below wisdom itself. He argued that 'no one would choose to live without friends, even if they had all other good things.'

Centuries later, the Stoic philosopher Seneca echoed the same truth.

He advised that while we must be self-reliant, we should never be solitary.

He believed friendship provided a mirror for self-understanding and a space for moral growth. 'Without a friend,' he wrote, 'no one would choose to live, though he had all other goods.'

Fast forward to the Enlightenment, and the Scottish philosopher David Hume, who argued that friendship was essential for both reason and virtue.

In his view, humans were not purely rational individuals but emotional beings whose feelings of sympathy bound us together. Hume believed that our moral sense, our very ability to tell right from wrong, arose from this sympathy.

Even modern existentialists, those famous for their emphasis on individuality, never dismissed the importance of social connection.

Jean-Paul Sartre, who is famous for his particularly pessimistic and individualistic outlook on the world, might have said, 'Hell is other people' but even he had to admit that meaning emerges in relationship to others.

On that note, I'm not sure out of all of histories philosophers I'd want Sartre round for Sunday lunch and a friendly chat. Also, he died in 1980, so I'm pretty sure he'd never reply to my invitation anyway. Frankly I'm relieved.

You see, every great philosophical tradition, from the Stoics of Greece to the Confucians of China, sees human flourishing as *relational*. Confucius talked about *ren* – often translated as 'humaneness' or 'benevolence'. To be fully human, he taught, was to act with kindness and respect in relationship. 'The benevolent person,' he said, 'loves others.'

The philosopher Alain de Botton, whose amazing organisation 'The School of Life' puts it succinctly: 'The good life is not a solo performance but a complex symphony of friendships, conversations, and shared experiences.'

Effectively, while our culture still tends to glorify independence and showcase the 'self-made person' the reality is that no man or woman is an island, and deep down we're super social animals.

In my own life, I've noticed that the times I've felt most grounded weren't when I'd achieved something impressive, but when I'd laughed over a pint with a mate or shared a walk with someone who'd listened, really listened, to what I was going through. The laughter, the listening, the shared moments, they're not insignificant. They're what it takes to live a life well-lived.

If the evidence points to the fact that social wellbeing is great for us and the great thinking, both ancient and modern, confirm this is the case, what insights have our great guests shared on social wellbeing?

Guests' Insights on the Importance of Social Wellbeing

One of the things I've learned about social wellbeing from interviewing loads of fantastic guests for this book is that habits matter.

Marc Eccles and I had a brilliant conversation about this where we spoke about the simple rule he makes himself.

'Chris, I never let a month pass without reaching out to someone who matters. The trick,' Marc told me, 'is to invest time reaching out to people you care about. It isn't about having loads of friends. It's about investing the time to keep the good ones in your orbit.'

I loved interviewing Nick Elston who spoke with frankness about anxiety, identity and connection particularly through his own lived experience. Nick told me that for years he'd worn a 'mask', pretending he was the confident professional while hiding how he was truly feeling.

'We talk about mental health like it's an individual thing,' Nick told me. 'However, the solution is social. Ultimately, it's about finding your tribe, the people you know you can communicate with without your mask.'

And Rebecca Wilson, author of *How to Have an Epic Retirement* talked about how, as we approached our fifties, sixties and beyond, we often focus on the financial challenges, but not the life ones. She said, 'You see, Chris, most people plan financially for retirement, but not emotionally. I think we need not only to consider how we're going to afford the retirement we want, but who we're going to spend it with.'

I couldn't agree more. This is a fundamental point of planning for what happens next.

So with that in mind, let's think about some practical ways we can improve our social wellbeing today.

Practical, Low-Cost Experiments to Improve Your Social Wellbeing

When it comes to building better social wellbeing, the good news is this: it doesn't require a big personality, a massive social calendar, or even much money. What it really needs is *intention* – the willingness to put connection back on the to-do list.

Here are a few small, evidence-backed experiments to try:

The One Action You Can Take to 'Be More Mike'

We've all got a 'Mike' or a 'Cassie' in our lives. Those who don't just mean to stay in touch, they actually do! The good news is that you can steal Mike and Cassie's superpower really simply without wearing a cape or your underwear over your trousers.

Do this one thing...

Every day, pick one person who matters and reach out.

A quick message, a shared link, a 'fancy a pint?' text. It's not about quantity. It's about rhythm. Do it for a month and see what happens.

Create a Club

Creating and being part of a 'club' doesn't need to be formal. I've got a bunch of friends in a group we call 'curry club' and once a month we get together for a curry, although the curry part sometimes happens and sometimes doesn't.

What always happens is loads of laughs, time spent with good people and relationships that deepen over time. Oh, and loads of in-jokes, mainly at my expense!

Thinking about it, I'm part of a bunch of clubs that are designed to maintain social connections. One club is 'Thursday club' (a little gang of us on a Thursday that play padel together), a lunch club, and a few more.

The good news is that creating a club doesn't need anything grander than a desire to get a bunch of good people together, and a way to do so, be in WhatsApp, text message, email or carrier pigeon (although carrier pigeon might be a tad inefficient!)

Making Time in Your Diary

'I'd love to make time to be more social, Chris,' you might choose to say, 'but I'm just too busy.'

I get it. I really do. Life, and everything else that comes with it, often gets in the way.

However, if the Jason and Dellis' story teaches us anything, it's this: Making a commitment on a regular basis and scheduling time in our diaries to spend time with people we love and like, and keeping that commitment, is one low-cost practical action.

My recommendation is to put it in the calendar like a work meeting and consider it an investment into your happiness and overall wellbeing.

The 'Three Message Sunday' Habit

Try this. Every Sunday evening, send three short messages to people you've lost touch with. It doesn't need to be anything fancy, just something like 'I Thought of you today,' 'How's life?' or 'We need to catch up soon.' You'll be amazed at how many of those little nudges turn into proper conversations.

Make Social Connection a Game

Often, I find that if I turn something into a game, I'm more than likely to perform actions to improve my wellbeing. So try this...

Write down ten people who matter to you, but you rarely see. Pop their names in a jar. Once a week, pull one out and give them a call or text to say hello and potentially arrange to meet up.

If you want to be a bit more technologically savvy than using a pen or paper there's also plenty of apps and websites that randomise names for you, including the website that does exactly what it says on the tin, the brilliantly titled Wheelofnames.com.

Basically, by gamifying the element of reaching out and setting yourself a challenge, it might provide you with the motivation you need to do so.

It sounds all too simple, doesn't it? Call a friend. Create a club. Message three people each Sunday.

If you're thinking this, you're right. However, these small social acts are minimal on their own, but can cumulate to something incredibly worthwhile. Less loneliness and a happier you.

Alternatively, some really, erm, rather interesting dad dancing might float your boat as it does mine. Asking questions of others and listening can maintain both our social wellbeing but also our sense of curiosity and intellectual wellbeing.

And...

Spending time with others to help your broader community, be it through fundraising, spending time improving a garden for a community group, or mentoring young people, means that your social and community wellbeing can complement each other perfectly.

Here's three practical ideas worth thinking about when considering...

Cooking With People You love and Like

Food is the original connector.

Invite a friend or neighbour around for a 'cook together' evening. It doesn't need to be a fancy dinner party, just a collaborative meal. You chop, they stir, you both talk.

Cooking with others has been shown to increase feelings of belonging and lower stress levels, and sharing the meal you've made can go one better. As we've already talked about in this book, cooking with fresh ingredients and being mindful of what you eat, is a great way to improve your nutrition.

Host a Learning Club

Gather three to five people to explore a shared interest, from photography to local history, philosophy to poetry. Rotate hosting duties and keep it informal. The goal isn't mastery but mutual curiosity.

This would provide a boost to both your social and intellectual wellbeing and potentially increase your sense of purpose.

Volunteer With a Friend

I've spoken to so many people who utilise their knowledge, skills and expertise to support others and volunteer their time. You can do this with a friend or solo. Either way, you should meet some amazing people who also support the charity.

My wife Cassie supports a homeless charity and, only last week, took her friend to volunteer too. The double win was the time they spent both together and helping others.

Applying the NEXT Model to Social Wellbeing

Like every wellbeing domain, social connection benefits from a bit of structure and we can use the **NEXT** model to give us that framework.

Navigate:

Start by taking an honest look at where you are right now. How connected do you really feel? Are there relationships you've let drift? Which connections give you energy – and which drain it? Write it down. Awareness is the first step.

Evaluate:

Ask yourself what kind of connections you want more of. Maybe it's rekindling old friendships, finding peers with shared interests, or building a sense of belonging in your local community. This is where you identify what 'enough' looks like socially.

eXecute:

Take one small, concrete action this week. Send a message, arrange a walk, join a group… volunteer. Momentum matters more than magnitude.

Track:

Reflect regularly on how these small steps make you feel. Do you feel more supported, more alive, more grounded? Notice what's working and what isn't – then adjust. Relationships, like gardens, flourish with attention.

When I think back to the version of me ten years ago: busy, driven, and quietly disconnected, I realise how easy it is to neglect social wellbeing in our lives. At certain times, other elements of our lives are guaranteed to get pretty busy.

Despite this, the evidence highlights the importance of having friendships to aid our wellbeing. Ancient and modern philosophers agree at the importance of social connections, and the practical things we can do to build stronger and deeper social connections in our lives,

Starting *The Kindness Project* with Charlotte taught me that connection isn't something you wait for – it's something you build. Week after week, chatting to guests, laughing with my daughter, I rediscovered the simple truth that relationships don't just add meaning to life – they *are* the meaning.

Often the reality isn't only the things we do in life. Sometimes it's about who is along with us for the ride. But maintaining those relationships takes work and my desire is, if you needed it, this chapter is a wake-up call to understand that social relationships often take work.

So make that call. Send that message. Arrange a coffee with that mate. I promise you, you'll feel a lot better for it.

In the next chapter I want to explore the role work is going to play in the next chapter of our lives.

Now, you might be saying to yourself 'it's not' and that might be the right answer for you. However, I want to make a case for continued work and the role it plays in a longer, happier, healthier life.

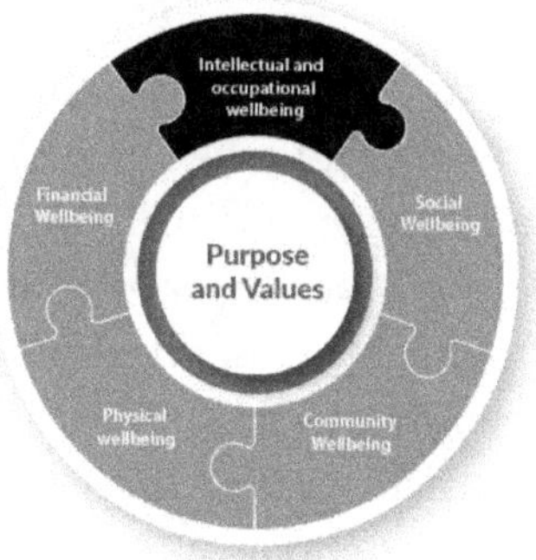

Chapter Seven

Intellectual and Occupational Wellbeing

'Choose a job you love, and you will never have to work a day in your life.' – Confucius

I want to tell you about my Uncle Jimmy.

Jimmy, like many men of his generation, went to work as a young man at a large East London-based industrial sugar manufacturer (rhyming with 'Mate and Piles') in an era where most people had one employer throughout their career.

So after a few decades, and with the benefit of a decent final salary pension and armed with the fact that he'd stopped enjoying the work, he decided to 'retire' early.

Initially, Jimmy loved retirement. No early starts. Complete freedom of time. Less stress. Then boredom set in. Jimmy needed a daily routine, something to replace the routine of work. For Jimmy, this new daily routine often involved a visit to the pub.

I haven't got a vendetta against pubs by the way. I'm known to frequent them every now and again. However, I'm not convinced that a daily visit to the pub when retired is a plan towards a healthier, happier retirement.

The challenge Jimmy faced is that with no routine in his life, and potentially the loss of purpose or meaning and contribution work provides us, Jimmy's health began to deteriorate.

Jimmy died in his late sixties, and I've got to be careful here. Correlation isn't causation and situations are always more complex and nuanced than this simple short story.

However, I'd suggest that loss of purpose, identity and community all contributed to this outcome.

Jimmy was unique, but his story isn't.

We've all got our own examples. Recently, I've been thinking, and talking to people about the traditional concept of 'retirement', with many recalling their own stories of how a conventional retirement didn't work.

The man who sold his business and died a year later. The inspirational head teacher who worked until her late sixties and passed away relatively soon after.

The man who had been looking forward to his first trip around the world but didn't live long enough to take it.

The dad and grandad, who since retiring, has become more withdrawn and depressed. The mum and nan who filled their time by constantly visiting the same three supermarkets in her town every day. I don't know about you but that sounds like a version of *Groundhog Day* I'm not planning to watch in a hurry.

Let's concentrate on another story. It's someone I've already mentioned at the start of this book: Mike. You may remember his journey from a senior engineering role for a large car company to realising he wasn't entirely ready for the retirement he once craved.

As a result, Mike sent me a photo of a model aeroplane accompanied by a text message suggesting that he should probably revisit his ideal version of the next chapter of his life. That, in turn, set me on a path to explore what we should consider in our fifties or sixties when we're thinking about our ideal 'what happens next'.

Mike's story, on the other hand, continued in a way you might not expect. Despite having achieved financial freedom and spending time doing things he loved, such as Mike walking his dog and painting, he did something interesting.

Mike went back to work.

Not in his old job. Not doing the same sort of hours or performing the same tasks he did previously.

But in work where he could use his skills, knowledge and expertise, but without some of the frustrations in his previous role.

You see, one of the things Mike loved about his work was his ability to educate and train young people. As he progressed through his career he found himself being promoted, and the satisfaction he got from doing the work decreased.

So in this chapter of his life, Mike chose how much he worked and, more importantly, chose the work he did, namely helping assess, train and guide apprentice engineers.

I remember chatting with Mike about the role work now plays in his life, and he told me something interesting.

'Chris, I thought work was something I had to do,' he said. 'Now, when I have the opportunity to choose challenging work that helps others and is enjoyable, it's something I get to do.'

I think there's a lot of wisdom in Mike's perspective on work. You see, I think the traditional perspective of retirement where we 'learn, earn, then rest' ignores something important: Our desire to maintain purpose and meaning in our lives, often through work.

I recently had the opportunity to interview Roland Butcher. Roland has had a fascinating career as the first black cricketer to represent England, then as a director of sports at the University of West Indies. Now as an author, commentator and mentor.

I interviewed Roland, along with one of the women he coached and mentored during his stint at the University of West Indies. Dr Sasha Sutherland is an incredibly impressive woman. She is now an educator and director of the Caribbean anti-doping organisation, ensuring the eighteen Caribbean member countries maintain high standards in their respective sports. Sasha also collaborated with Roland to tell his story in his recently published book. Interestingly, this has ignited a desire to do more storytelling in her own life.

We talked about the roles we play throughout our life as mentors and mentees. Then the conversation turned to the old-fashioned model of retirement and Roland, who is now in his early seventies and where work remains an important part of his life, had an interesting perspective.

'Chris, I think that learn, earn and then rest is a model that doesn't work for a lot of people anymore. I see it slightly differently. My life's journey is about learning, earning and then giving back. I'm now in the era of my life where I get to give back.'

I love this perspective. What if, like both Mike and Roland, the next chapter of our lives isn't simply about relaxation, but about the opportunity to do more of what we love? In doing so, we can maintain our curiosity and engagement in the world, keep our minds moving forward, and continue to find meaningful ways to help others.

So, stories of my uncle Jimmy potentially suggest that stopping work to take the conventional route to retirement isn't particularly good for our health or well-being. On the flip side, Mike and Roland's choice to continue working – on their own terms – as part of their lives might lead to a greater wellbeing. However, what does the evidence say?

Is work – however we choose to define it in later life – good for us? Are we happier when we continue to work? And how do we, in a stage of our lives where we may be aiming to strive for a better balance, ensure that our relationship with work helps makes us happier rather than more miserable.

Let's take a look...

What Does the Evidence Say About the Role Work Plays in Our Lives?

The evidence on whether continued work is good for us is interesting... It depends on the work.

You see, many studies show beneficial outcomes when work continues to play a part in our later lives, but how your work, what you do and, really importantly, why you continue to work are all fundamentally important.

A huge study of adults over fifty showed that 71% said work had a positive impact on mental health, with those sixty-five and older being more positive about the role work played in their lives.

Nevertheless, the nature of the work we choose to do has a fundamental impact. A 2017 study found that we value work when it is meaningful, flexible, intellectually stimulative and social.

The research showed that the quality of the job mattered

based on how much we get out of work. High-stress, low-autonomy work could actually have a negative impact on our mental and physical health. That's why when we're thinking about the role work plays in the next chapter of our lives, it's not about any work, but work that we control, which we value and challenges us enough, without causing negative stress.

Another important element is the amount of time we spend at work. The happiest 'next chapter' person continued to work but had a far better work-life balance. The job doesn't dominate how we spend our time.

So, does the evidence suggest that work – and the intellectual challenge that comes with it – is good for us?

The short answer is 'yes'. However, it does depend on a number of factors, including the quality of our job, how much autonomy we have, how meaningful we find our work, how stressful it is, and how much flexibility we have.

The evidence also shows that work makes us happier when we decide how to spend our time doing it. This might include some paid work, but could also be volunteering, mentoring, and learning new skills, as well as a decent chunk of time simply enjoying life.

This balance means that by adhering to the status quo of full-time work, or stopping immediately, we design a life that works for us and allows us to get a decent degree of balance in our lives.

As I write this, the world of work continues to change. New technologies have been introduced and continue to reshape what work means. Yet all the evidence suggests that when our work provides meaning, purpose, flexibility, autonomy and intellectual stimulation, it makes us happier and healthier people.

We are living in a world, particularly in our working lives, that is changing faster than ever before. But are there any constants throughout human history that can offer insight into the nature of work? Is there wisdom from the deepest thinkers that might guide us toward finding work to enhance our lives?

Let's look at how both ancient and modern philosophers view the role of work and how it plays in our lives...

What Did the Philosophers Say About the World of Work?

Most philosophers agree that a good life includes a degree of intellectual effort.

We've already explored that the concept of 'retirement' is one that came to prominence in the industrial age. For as long as humans have been on the planet, the majority of us would have continued working until they were physically unable to do so.

So, looking to the philosophers for inspiration on retirement is interesting. It's likely that they wouldn't have understood our obsession with stopping work at a particular age.

In fact, if you tried to explain to Plato the concept of 'retirement' it's likely he would have laughed so much he would have spilt his goblet of wine over his Toga.

Personally, I believe that there are several things we can learn from both ancient and modern-day philosophy, and how work might play a part in our future decisions.

You see, both ancient and modern philosophy discuss the importance of doing something (we believe will be) positive with our lives and continually improving how we do it. The Stoics, in particular, talked about 'choosing your labours wisely'. In other words, doing work which really matters to you.

Also, both ancient and modern philosophers agree that purposeful activity and ongoing mental challenge play an important part in wellbeing later in our lives.

Aristotle had some brilliant insights when he talked about Eudemonia. This is the concept of living in alignment with our values, purpose and potential. We do this by pursuing goals that express our true self, allow us to develop our abilities, and contribute to something larger and more important to ourselves. For me, meaningful work can make a huge contribution to this.

Confucius emphasised the importance of lifelong learning as a practice, and it's in our power to continue to learn and challenge ourselves intellectually regardless of our age. Confucius also talked about the importance of mentoring later in our lives, something that in the modern world is exemplified by the likes of Roland, whose story I told earlier in this chapter.

Other modern thinkers, like Scottish American philosopher Alasdair MacIntyre talk about 'practice' as a socially rooted activity where the focus isn't what you get paid (an external reward) but where the rewards are intrinsic. You continue to learn, to get better and to continue to serve others.

Richard Sennett, the American sociologist, agrees and describes continuing work as part of our lives – a desire to do a job well for its own sake, for deep satisfaction and, ultimately, keep our brains and bodies active.

There are loads of great conversations on the *What Happens Next* podcast, particularly about the role that continued work plays in our lives.

If you're thinking about the role that continued work plays in your life, I'd recommend you watch Jon Dunkley. In this interview, Jon shares his insights into wellbeing and the three elements we need for balance. For many of us thinking about 'what happens next' we need to find more time for doing the stuff we love. However, we all know that hedonism, doing stuff we simply find fun, is an important consideration in our future happiness. Jon talks about the need to strike the right balance between hedonism, eudamonism (life with purpose) and chthonic wellbeing (experiencing awe in life).

You can find Jon's interview here....

I also found deep inspiration from retired heart surgeon Tom Spyt. He speaks about the feeling of loss when his age stopped him doing something he loved. During our interview we talk about how he's replaced this feeling with renewed purpose through his new occupation.

You can find Tom's interview here...

And...

Hilary Rowland and Peter Hyson speak about how they rearrange their time by blending learning, helping others and continuing to do professional work, but with a balance that works perfectly for them.

You can hear a lot more about Hilary and Peter's story here...

Now you've heard about the insights my amazing expert guests have shared, let's get practical and talk about how we apply low-cost experiments in the next chapter of our lives to find work that improves our wellbeing. Work which provides autonomy, meaning, purpose and social connection.

What small incremental steps can we take to get closer to the work we actually want to do?

Small Experiments to Get You Closer to Work You Love and How to Avoid the Retirement Cliff

For generations, retirement was imagined as a single event: a moment where one day you are working, and the next day you are not. For many people, and possibly you, that sharp cut-off was psychologically brutal.

I sometimes describe it to clients as 'the retirement cliff': the sudden absence of structure, stimulation, and social contact that can catch people unprepared.

The cliff is risky – not only financially but emotionally. There is often a risk that, almost overnight, you lose many of the ingredients that supported your sense of identity and intellectual challenge.

When I talk to clients about this, I introduce a retirement flight path instead. This is a gradual, purposeful descent into a new landscape, not a plunge off a cliff into the great unknown and towards the earth with a significant bump.

A flight path lets you experiment a bit more. For many of my clients this includes a gradual process, where they work out how they'd like to spend their time, either involving work or not, in the next chapter of their lives.

One of the most successful strategies I've seen work time and time again is treating the transition to the next chapter as several small, deliberate experiments, rather than a single irreversible decision.

However, the first small action you should consider take to find work you love is deceptively simple.

You should *make room to decide.*

Block out one non-negotiable day – or even half a day – as your 'pilot project' time. Have the necessary conversation to protect that space, ensuring you have the time and headspace to focus on it fully.

During that time, you don't do your old job, your errands, or your chores. You explore. You read, write, volunteer, call an interesting person, or visit a workplace you're curious about.

Use this space not to decide, but to explore what you might want to include in the next chapter of your life from a work perspective.

In my experience, if you don't create a bit of space in your week for this, the danger is you carry on what you're doing for a lot longer than is healthy, simply because you've not given yourself the time to reflect on what else you might choose to do.

The second practical low-cost experiment is also deceptively simple.

Try some new stuff!

In many of the videos we share on the *What Happens Next* YouTube channel we talk about designing our future lives through a series of micro experiments where you can simply try stuff out.

There's plenty of ways this can be achieved. For example, you could shadow someone doing a role you're curious about for a day.

Or…

Teach your skills and knowledge to a group of people who would benefit. This might include young people, people in your profession, or fellow 'what happens nexters'.

By reducing the time in your day job you could use the space you've created to volunteer one morning a week at a local charity or school, but with two important conditions…

Firstly, I'd always suggest spending your time supporting an organisation you care about and does fine work. Secondly, it's worth thinking about something that stretches your skills but doesn't give you too much stress.

You could join a short online course and focus on a skill you've always thought about doing but never had the time. Examples from my clients include photography, coding and developing additional skills, to become a better storyteller. My wife has recently decided that she wants to become better at pottery and has produced some amazing things that now decorate our home.

You could build a short-term mentoring relationship with

a generation or a couple of generations younger than you, sharing your knowledge and expertise to support them with the challenges they face.

There's some amazing mentoring organisations in the UK that are worth checking out, particularly the 'grandmentors' scheme, which you can find at www.volunteeringmatters.org.uk, the youth charity, MCR (www.mcrpathways.org) or the one million mentors project (https://onemillionmentors.org.uk/)

The point is not to make decisions immediately. Instead, focus on what you enjoy, how you add value, and where the balance lies between what you can do well and what continues to stretch and challenge you. As you run these experiments, play closer attention to when you feel energised, useful and curious, and when you feel drained or indifferent.

Then, if you include more of what you love, and less of what you don't, over time you might work out what you like to do in the next chapter of your life.

Another important thing you can do – for no cost but with a little effort – is to tell yourself a different story about work.

Most people, consciously or not, carry a narrow definition of work. Often, for many, it's something you get paid to do between nine and five. But when you look closely at people who flourish in their sixties and seventies, their definition is far wider.

They treat 'work' as purposeful application. Using skills, attention and effort in service of something that matters.

That could be paid consulting, mentoring, board service, artistic creation, activism, or caring. For many as they move into the next chapter of their lives it's a combination of a lot of these. In my opinion, there are three questions worth asking to widen your own definition of work...

- First, where do I still feel curious?
- Second, who could benefit from what I already know?
- And last, but definitely not least, what would I still do if no one paid me?

If there is an overlap with those three, you've found a candidate for your next piece of work. We've already spoken about the fact that one of the hardest parts of the transition from full-time work isn't financial – it's **identity.**

When someone asks, 'What do you do?' and you're no longer sure of the answer, it can feel destabilising. The trick is to rehearse your new identity before you need it.

So the low-cost experiment worth thinking about is this...

When someone new asks what you do, try answering in a way that reflects where you're heading, not where you've been.

For example: 'I'm moving into mentoring young engineers,' or 'I'm exploring creative education.'

Then all you need to do is notice how it feels to say it. Does it feel like an identity you can step into? If so, what's the incremental next step to see if this actually fits?

Evidence does show that we benefit from continual learning, particularly in our middle and later lives. In my opinion, the other thing that is broken about the traditional 'learn, earn, then stop' model is that we know that lifelong curiosity and learning is brilliant for our own mental health and wellbeing.

Intellectual wellbeing thrives when we continually learn. You don't have to enrol in a degree. Small, structured learning keeps the brain active and curiosity high.

Also, as we've talked about throughout this chapter. If you want to learn more, become a teacher or mentor. Both our guests on the podcast agree that a decent chunk of the evidence validate what the ancient Stoic philosopher Seneca the younger said millennia ago, 'If you want to learn, teach.'

Wellbeing Stacking to Improve Our Occupational and Intellectual Wellbeing

There are plenty of brilliant ways to combine wellbeing at work with other aspects of your overall health and fulfilment.

The work that involves engaging with new people allows you to build new relationships and potentially improve your social wellbeing. If these opportunities require you to move your body, they could potentially improve your physical wellbeing.

If you're going to become a mentor, it might be worth having a mentoring conversation while having a stroll in the park instead of sitting still, or listening to a podcast while at the gym.

If the work you do improves the world, this can significantly improve your wellbeing in the community and provide you with a massive sense of purpose.

It's interesting.

If you're lucky enough to find work you love, it's often because it improves our wellbeing in a range of different ways.

However, the big question here is to find and do more of the work we truly love.

Here's where I believe that the NEXT model can play an important part in supporting you to do this.

Using the N.E.X.T Model to Improve Your Occupational and Intellectual Wellbeing

So how do we find or do work we love?

The good news is that there's a clear framework in the **N.E.X.T** model which gets you closer to the work you can truly do.

Navigate to Improve Your Occupational and Intellectual Wellbeing

That starts with navigation. Working out what ideal work looks like for you, where you can ask yourself a number of questions...

- When have you felt the proudest in your working life?
- What are you still curious about?
- What specific activities feel like work to everyone else, but don't feel like work to you?

Then it's worth looking at being slightly more practical. How many hours per week would you ideally like to spend at work? What days would be ideal days to work? Are there any 'non negotiables' when it comes to finding work you love?

Once you've considered these questions, it should give you a better idea of what good work looks like for you.

The next step is to **Evaluate** where you are today, and you can do this by answering the following questions?

- How close is the work you do now and the ideal work you've laid out when going through the navigation step?
- What's the big differences?
- Out of ten, how does your current work rank in relation to providing you with autonomy, meaning, the opportunity to learn, social connections and stress?

Next, we begin taking action – moving you closer to work and learning you truly love by starting to **eXecute**.

We've already talked about this earlier in the chapter, but the first thing you should do is carve out sometime in your diary as a non-negotiable period where you can start performing small incremental experiments.

This will give you both some thinking time, but also an opportunity to try different work and learning opportunities you can experiment with.

Then map out a few of these low-cost experiments. You might try tutoring for a few weeks to see whether that might be a part of your next chapter work life. You might want to spend a few weeks learning a brand-new subject. Alternatively, you might want to set up a short-term project using the time you've carved out to do something you're really interested in. That project could be anything which uses the skills you've got for a cause or interest you love.

This could range from helping a local charity out by clearing debris from their garden because you love manual work and being outdoors, to writing a novella because you love telling stories all the way through to helping a classroom of kids with a financial education program (something I've had the privilege of doing).

The objective here is not to find the thing you want to do instantly, but to try things out in order to figure out what work looks like for you in the next chapter of your life.

Now it's time to keep **Track.**

My recommendation is every time you try an experiment you rank it using the following questions...

- Does this work or learning feel purposeful?
- How much autonomy have I got doing this?
- How much stress do I feel when performing this task?
- How does this work contribute to the human connection I really value?

Then use these answers to continuously **Navigate, Evaluate, eXecute** and **Track** to get you closer to the work you love.

Often when we're finding work we love, it's because we're making an evolution in the way we see the world in our fifties and sixties.

I know that personally that my perception of what success looks like for me has definitely changed.

When I first started my business, I knew I had to survive. Then I wanted to make sure my business remained sustainable. Now, I think a lot more about significance.

Significance can mean a lot of things. However, for me it's all about making a positive contribution, and our next chapter is all about exploring what that means in the next chapter of our lives.

We're going to call it 'Community Wellbeing'...

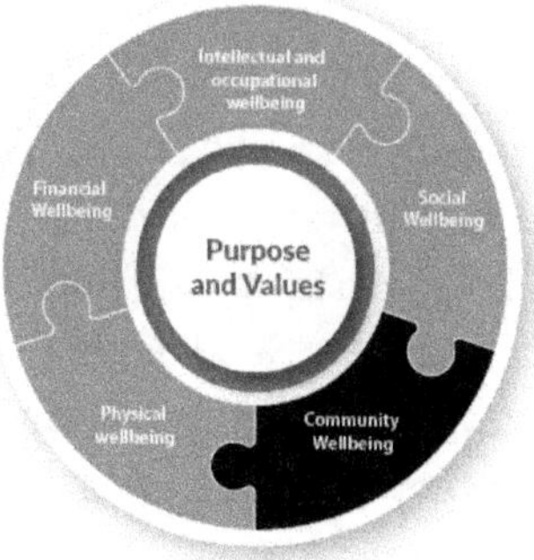

Chapter Eight

Community Wellbeing

'The best way to find yourself is to lose yourself in the service of others.' – Mahatma Gandhi

Come rain or shine, every day across the country thousands of people lace up their trainers and meet up for a run, walk or cycle.

That being said, the people I've got in mind aren't just part of a running, walking or cycling club. They're part of something I'd suggest that's slightly bigger. They're part of a UK-wide movement called Goodgym, an organisation designed to help people both 'Get fit' and 'Do good'.

I first heard about Goodgym a few years ago when a friend of mine, Patrick Luong, shared his love for the organisation. He liked the fact that they combine two things that make his life better. Helping others and staying fit.

Every day UK Goodgym embrace initiatives that combine fitness with community. For instance, today there's a cycle to a homeless shelter, in which the 'Goodgymers' help feed the homeless. Tomorrow there's a walk, combined with a litter pick. The next day there's a run to an older vulnerable person's house, where she will be helped to trim her plants.

All over the country the 'Goodgymers' combine staying fit and doing good. Over a hundred thousand acts of kindness shows us something powerful when we're thinking about what happens next in our lives...

Doing good for others is good for us.

I spoke earlier about my experience interviewing Roland Butcher, the UK's first black cricketer. I asked him how the conventional idea of retirement of "Learn, Earn and Rest" might be broken.

Roland, now in his early seventies, had a different perspective. 'I don't want to rest Chris,' he told me. I'm not in the position to have learned, earned, and want to return.'

I asked him what he meant about 'returning', He just said he wanted to make a positive contribution to the world. It's all about supporting, encouraging and mentoring amazing people. It's all about giving back.

I often speak about the phases I've gone through in my life. Looking back to my early thirties – a time when I started my business, alongside having a mortgage and a young family – life felt insecure. This felt to me like a period of survival.

Then after a few years, it felt that I was building things in myself. My business and family were on stronger foundations and it was time to build on this sustainability.

I now feel like I'm moving into a period fundamentally different – a period of significance. I'm now looking over the next few decades and wondering how I can make more of a positive impact on the world?

Not in a grand way. I'm no Mother Theresa. I wouldn't look good in the Sari for a start. Despite this, I'm looking at how to make a more positive dent in the universe, before I leave the planet for good.

I often find myself having conversations with clients, friends and *What Happens Next?* interviewees about this too. People who, in their own ways, are striving to leave the planet a slightly better place than they found it.

This can be as simple as helping members of their family or by giving their time, effort and energy to causes they believe in.

Still, before we run away with ourselves, let's look at the evidence. Will doing good for others in our communities (regardless of how we define 'community') improve our happiness and wellbeing.

Is There Evidence for Community Wellbeing When You're Thinking About 'What Happens Next'?

Psychologists have long recognised a phenomenon known as the 'helper's high'. First documented by Allan Luks in the 1980s, it describes the surge of positive emotion people feel after doing something kind or generous.

Luks surveyed thousands of volunteers and found that over ninety per cent, after helping someone, reported physical and emotional calmness, as well as increased energy and self-worth.

Subsequent studies, using MRI scans, confirmed that altruistic acts activate the same brain regions associated with reward and pleasure – particularly the ventral striatum and prefrontal cortex.

In other words, doing good 'feels good' because our brains are wired for it. When we help, we trigger the release of endorphins, oxytocin, and dopamine, the exact same chemicals that promote connection, reduce stress, and even strengthen immune responses.

Researchers at the University of Exeter analysed data from forty studies involving fifty thousand participants and found that those who volunteered regularly were significantly more likely to report higher life satisfaction and lower rates of depression than those who didn't. The link remained strong even when allowing for income, education, and baseline wellbeing.

This pattern isn't limited to formal volunteering. Everyday acts like checking in on a neighbour, donating to charity, or mentoring a colleague produce the same emotional and physiological rewards.

The Paradox of Self-Interest

It's tempting to think of helping as 'something we do for others', but the data shows it also fulfils deep psychological needs of our own. Self-determination theory, developed by psychologists Edward Deci and Richard Ryan, identifies three core needs that drive wellbeing: autonomy, competence, and relatedness.

The good news is that helping others meets all three...

When we choose to give, we exercise autonomy and act in alignment with our values. We feel competent when we make a difference. And we experience relatedness through connection and shared purpose. That combination makes helping a powerful antidote to loneliness and disconnection.

Basically, the more we focus on others, the more personally fulfilled we become. This 'paradox of self-interest' explains why communities built on reciprocity, where giving and receiving coexist, tend to thrive. The evidence suggests that helping others as an individual improves personal wellbeing, but helping others in a group helps multiply the effect and means that you get to live in nicer neighbourhoods.

A 2019 UK Government study on community life found that areas with higher volunteering and mutual-aid participation also reported higher levels of trust, lower crime, and greater life satisfaction. Even modest involvement, attending local events or chatting with neighbours, correlates with stronger perceptions of safety and belonging.

The Marmot Review on Health Inequalities (2020) reinforced this point: social participation is one of the strongest determinants of both physical and mental health. The more cohesive the community, the healthier and happier its residents. This suggests that kindness and connection aren't simply moral choices. They're ways to live longer, happier and healthier lives.

So by undertaking positive action to help others and becoming far more engaged in our communities, this is something that can positively impact your 'what happens next' plan.

But did the ancient and modern-day philosophers agree on this concept?

The Philosophical Take on Community Wellbeing

Ancient philosophy anticipated what modern science now confirms, especially with regards to positive personal impact we receive from helping others.

Aristotle talked a lot about eudaemonia (human flourishing). He inferred that it does not come primarily from pleasure or wealth, but from helping others. 'To live well,' he said, 'is to contribute to the *polis*, the wider social fabric.'

Confucius expressed a similar view: 'The man of humanity, wishing to establish himself, also establishes others.'

Centuries later, the philosopher Martin Buber described life as an 'I–Thou' relationship – our identity shaped through encounters of mutual respect and care.

These traditions converge on a single idea: meaning is relational. We become who we are through what we give to others.

I was really fortunate to explore a lot of themes in my last book, *The Kindness Project*. In the book I talk a bit about how often kindness is seen as soft and intangible. My experience is that often the benefits of kindness are widespread – bringing communities together, improving social trust, and encouraging more people to help out and get involved.

Effectively, the philosophers and the evidence are aligned. Being actively involved in our communities, and kind to others, is brilliant for our mental health and is something we should certainly consider when thinking about the next chapter of our lives.

The brilliant guests featured on *What Happens Next* have all made positive contributions, or built their own, communities.

Pete Matthew, founder of Meaningful Money, talked about his desire to share knowledge about money, has built a movement, not an audience. Pete found that by sharing his insights as a chartered financial planner he has built an amazing community of people who unite with a desire to learn and understand more, but also to support each other on their journeys.

You can find Pete's interview here...

Damian Stancombe spoke about his experience on the Camino de Santiago, an ancient pilgrimage route across northern Spain, and how one of the most meaningful aspects of the journey was the accidental community he formed along the way.

You see, Damian assumed that he did the walk to spend some time alone with his thoughts. He was seeking clarity on the next stage of his life and felt that walking the Camino trail might give him the time and headspace to allow him to do this.

Interestingly, Damian found himself walking with people who were on a similar journey. Along the walk, the temporary community of Camino trail walkers helped him put his 'what happens next' into greater perspective.

You can find Damian's interview here...

Penny and Thomas Power talked about the difference between a network and a community, and how their shift – particularly as they headed into their sixties – is mostly about belonging. During our interview, we spoke about the digital economy, and how it's based on 'followers' and 'likes'. In contrast, being part of, and contributing to a community, is based on trust.

Penny talked about emotional safety, and how for her, being part of a community was often when members feel they can be seen, heard and importantly valued.

You can find Penny and Thomas's interview on the next page...

However, as we've learned from the previous chapters, any improvement in wellbeing needs to be focused on positive action, so let's explore the incremental action you can take to improve your community wellbeing today.

Practical, Low-Cost Experiments for Building Community Wellbeing

The brilliant thing about community wellbeing is that it doesn't require huge donations, political movements or vast amounts of spare time. Most of what builds stronger connections can be done for free, in small, regular doses.

So here are a few ideas to try...

Once a month, pick one local group to visit. A community garden, a litter-pick, a choir, a GoodGym run. See if you like it and if so start to attend a bit more regularly.

Alternatively, start a community based on something you are interested in. I've found myself curating a community of padel tennis players. But yours could be a coffee morning, a book swap, or an online meet-up for people exploring mid-life transitions. The act of convening people I've found turbo charges my community wellbeing.

If time is tight, micro-volunteering platforms like *Be My Eyes* or *Do-It* offer ten-minute opportunities like reading for the visually impaired, translating a document for a charity, or mentoring via email.

Or…

Choose one simple goal each month that improves your immediate area: plant wildflowers, tidy a shared space, or start a library of things. Invite neighbours to help. Shared effort builds local pride and, over time, trust.

How to Stack Community Wellbeing With Other Areas of Wellbeing

Earlier I mentioned Goodgym and how this perfectly combines doing good for others and staying fit in one neat little package.

It also perfectly describes Damian's Camino walk story, where he paired a very long walk with meeting new people. The good news is that you don't need a Spanish trek to combine physical and community wellbeing.

Instead, you can meet a friend or new acquaintance for a weekly walk. You could join a walking club or start your own walking club. You could start your own sports-based community like my padel Whatsapp group.

Regardless of what you choose, doing something which is good for your body and mind, combined with spending time helping others or engaging with your local community, can lead to more open conversations than sitting face-to-face.

We've spoken about one of the best ways to continue to improve your intellectual or occupational wellbeing is to teach, and this can allow you to take what you know and help the community learn this skill. I've personally volunteered to teach financial education at schools, but another great way to combine both community and intellectual wellbeing is a local 'skills swap'.

This is where you offer one of your skills to someone who needs it. You might choose to learn something from them, or simply ask them to pass the favour on. Either way, you're learning by teaching and feeling good by helping someone else.

Alternatively, one way to enhance your community wellbeing and remain engaged in life is by starting a book club.

I know that a lot of clients I've worked with find purpose, and improve their community wellbeing through mentoring or coaching others who need it.

The big question when we're thinking about the intersection between community wellbeing and other areas of wellbeing is, 'What could I do this month that would improve my own wellbeing and someone else's?'

If you can answer this, it's likely you've got a decent way to experiment with the next thing you might want to try?

Community Wellbeing and the NEXT Framework

Throughout this book, we've used the **NEXT** model, **Navigate, Evaluate, eXecute, Track**, to turn insight into action. Here's how it applies when you're building community wellbeing into your next chapter...

Navigate – Map Your Circles

- Start by noticing where community already exists in your life.
- Who are the people or groups that give you energy?
- Which spaces – digital or physical – make you feel safe and valued?
- Where do you see gaps?

Sketch your 'connection map': family, friends, neighbours, professional circles, causes, faith groups, hobbies. Seeing it on paper highlights both your strengths and your missing links.

Evaluate – Choose Your Mode of Contribution

Not everyone contributes in the same way.

- Are you a Connector (bringing people together), a Doer (helping practically), or a Guide (sharing wisdom and mentoring)?
- How much time and energy can you realistically give right now?

  Evaluating your preferred mode ensures that what you do feels energising rather than draining.

eXecute – Start Small, Stay Consistent

Pick one low-cost experiment from earlier and commit to it for a month. Consistency is what turns activity into community. Remember what Penny Power said about trust, 'It's built through showing up.'

Even a short, regular contribution – a weekly run, a monthly call – matters more than occasional grand gestures.

Track – Notice the Ripple Effects

Keep a brief journal or reflection each week...

- When did I feel most connected this week?
- What difference did I make, however small?
- What did I learn about myself from contributing?

Over time you'll see the ripple: better mood, broader network, stronger sense of purpose. You'll also start to spot opportunities to expand – perhaps combining your community efforts with another wellbeing goal or collaborating with someone new.

In the last few chapters, we've looked at finding and renewing purpose as we approach the next part of our lives, and the importance of financial, physical, social, intellectual and community wellbeing.

A lot of the ideas we've spoken about already might sound like statements of the bleedin' obvious. This raises an important question...

If we know what areas of our life we might want to improve and refine in the next chapter of our lives, what's stopping us?

Often, it's fear. Often, it's the fact that for your own unique version of 'what happens next' isn't written yet, and perfectly naturally, that's pretty scary.

So that's what the next chapter is all about. It's all about the first steps you should take to transition to the next chapter of your life. It's less 'what happens next' and more...

Chapter Nine

So What Happens Now?

'We make a living by what we get, but we make a life by what we give.' – Winston Churchill

I've asked a lot of questions in this book. Questions we tend to ask ourselves when we're in the messy middle of our lives. It's when the kids are either grown up, or getting there, and when our parents, if we're fortunate enough to still have them in our lives, are getting older.

It's when we've built successful careers or businesses, but, despite often being proud of where you are, after all the decades of building something, you start to wonder.

Is This All There Is?

The answer to this question, if you allow it, is always no. I'm a firm believer that if you're not entirely satisfied with where you are today, you've got the chance to make some positive change in your own life.

However, if you agree with me and we can make positive

change in our lives, you'll also realise that you've only just started the process of asking questions of yourself. The next big question for many people is...

What Happens Next?

This question is often a scary one. Mapping out the next couple of decades of your life, including thinking about what's going to make you happy, feels way too overwhelming for most of us.

Now, hopefully, I've shared some insights that allow you to make positive change today. I would suggest you use low-cost experimentation to help you work out what you want to include in the next chapter of your life and what you don't.

So when you're starting out on the journey to 'what happens next' there's a question to ask that acts as the perfect stepping stone...

What Happens Now?

You see, as humans, we're not great at planning our lives for the longer term.

Our brains have evolved to live and survive for today. Don't blame me though. Blame your caveman ancestors.

It's why so many of us, including many of my clients, make promises to our future selves. Some of these promises people never keep until it's too late.

We promise ourselves to volunteer 'next year', travel 'when we have more time', or 'get fit after things calm down'.

The problem is that next year isn't guaranteed. Things only calm down in your life when you're intentional about it.

There's a quote often misattributed to Seneca: 'If a man does not know to what port he is steering; no wind is favourable.'

Drift is the silent thief of midlife. It creeps in when things are 'fine'. Where work's okay, relationships are steady, the mortgage is manageable. Nothing's wrong, but nothing's thrilling either.

When we drift, we stop asking questions. We live on autopilot.

That's why reflection and recalibration – the core of your **NEXT** framework we've talked about through this book – is so powerful.

It provides you with a structure to ask ourselves questions as move you forward, while giving yourself the flexibility to provide answers that matter to you.

So, as often as you need to, and I'd suggest at least once a month, my recommendation is to ask yourself these questions.

- **Navigate**: Am I still heading in a direction that excites me?
- **Evaluate**: What's giving me energy? What's draining it?
- **eXecute**: What's one small thing I can do this week to move toward the life I want?
- **Track**: How will I know if it's working? What feedback am I getting from my mind, body, and relationships?

The goal here is to avoid drifting. You should be intentional as you move into the next chapter of your life – gradually and incrementally – toward a life you truly want to live.

What is Success to You?

One of the most liberating shifts that happens as we move through our fifties and sixties is that success becomes less about accumulation and more about alignment.

When I ask clients or interviewees what success means now, knowing they have enough money is an important factor, but one which diminishes in importance the more financially secure they feel.

Beyond the money, the conversations I often have with clients focus on how we measure our lives less by how high we climb and more by how deeply we live.

Aristotle would have recognised this as eudaimonia – flourishing through virtue, through meaningful action. It's success as congruence. In other words, living in a way that matches your values.

So What's Your Story?

Maybe you started this book feeling uncertain. About retirement, about change, about identity. Maybe you picked it up looking for reassurance or ideas.

Every story we've explored from GoodGym runners to Camino walkers to Mike's story, they are all fundamentally different, although they do share some interesting traits.

They all have a desire to make positive change in their own lives. A shift where success means a lot more than financial wealth and high status at work. This can include the frustration and difficult process of change, as well as a redefinition of what 'success' looks like.

If you've made it this far, your own story is probably shifting. The Stoics had a phrase *Amor Fati* (love of fate), which means accepting whatever happens not with resignation, but with enthusiasm.

The great modern-day philosopher and world champion boxer, Mr Mike Tyson, put it best when he said, 'Everyone's got a plan, until they get punched in the face.'

That's why, as you navigate the next chapter of your life, you don't need a perfect plan. Why? Because there's never a perfect time.

The step we need to take is a small one. Then another small one. Then another. Then again. Until we truly want to live in the next chapter of our lives.

Also, when things go wrong, and they will, we revisit the **NEXT** framework.

We **Navigate** – Work out where we want to go to improve our wellbeing in a specific part of our lives.

We **Evaluate** – by understanding where we are today.

We **eXecute** – by taking small, incremental actions and experiments to get marginally closer to where we want to be.

And...

We **Track** – We start the process again, ensuring we're still heading in the right direction, making progress and continuing to take the right action in the right direction.

But here's the truth I've seen time and again...

You Don't Have to Figure it Out Alone.

Even the most self-aware person has moments when reflection isn't enough. We all reach points when we need perspective, accountability, and encouragement.

We'll look at the kinds of support that make the biggest difference: the conversations worth having, the experts worth involving, and the companions who'll help you navigate, evaluate, eXecute, and track your progress with greater clarity and confidence.

If you've taken what you need from this book and don't believe you need any help to effectively navigate the next chapter of your life, and I applaud you if you can. Feel free to skip the next chapter.

However, if you're like me and believe that creating your version of 'what happens next' can be a team sport, let's take a look at who you might want on your team…

Chapter Ten

Who Can Help You with Your 'What Happens Next'?

'The secret of getting ahead is getting started.' – Mark Twain

Arnold Schwarzenegger tells a story in his recent book *Be Useful* that surprised me. In fact, the entire book surprised me. I thought I knew a lot about Arnie, but I think I underestimated how his life experiences had provided him with some pretty incredible insights.

Don't get me wrong. I know Schwarzenegger has made a bunch of mistakes in his life, which he openly admits in the book, but there are a few life lessons that I think are worth learning from.

Now, just so you know, every sinew in my body is trying to resist writing some Arnie-based puns here. So I'm not going to suggest you have 'total recall' on the things you used to love as a kid to help you inform what you want to do in your future – so you can, ahem, 'terminate' the things you don't enjoy and do more of what you love... even if that means pretending you're in 'kindergarten'. Or a 'cop'.

I'll get my coat.

The interesting thing about *Be Useful* is many of the stories aren't dramatic or full of Hollywood flair, but because often they're simply and brutally honest.

He describes growing up in Austria, dreaming impossibly big dreams: becoming the strongest man in the world, moving to America, becoming a movie star, and, later, a governor. Most people hear that journey and call it the ultimate 'self-made man' story.

But Arnold refuses the label.

In the book, he makes the point clearly: there is no such thing as a self-made man. Every achievement he's ever had – every door he's ever gone through – was opened, nudged, or widened by someone else. His parents. His first weightlifting coach. The bodybuilders who introduced him to LA. The agents who took a chance on his accent and name. The voters who put him in office.

His message is blunt: You can work incredibly hard, but no one builds a life alone.

But let's be frank. It's difficult to ask for help. Particularly when we've got years of experience, knowledge and wisdom.

However, if you're like me, you'll appreciate that with any challenge, change is made a lot easier with a bit of help. From our family. From our friends. From our mentors, and potentially from people who can provide unique insights.

Who's Going to Help You with Your 'What Happens Next' Journey?

The truth is, while self-reflection is vital, transformation rarely happens in isolation. A lot of this book is about looking inward. It's about asking questions of yourself. However, this chapter is about looking outward towards the people, communities, and collaborations that can help you live your next chapter with more clarity, confidence, and connection.

That's why, when people navigate retirement, career change, or big life shifts successfully, they rarely do it solo. They build a *team*. A small, trusted circle that offers perspective, structure, and support.

Think of this next phase less like a solo expedition and more like a voyage with guides. You're still the one steering the ship, but you'll sail further, faster, and more safely with the right crew beside you.

The Five People to Consider to Include On Your 'What Happens Next' Team

Over the years, I've come to believe there are five key people who make the biggest difference when you're planning the next chapter of your life.

Let's meet them...

Your Partner

If you share your life with someone: a spouse, partner, or even a close friend who feels like family, they should be the first person in the conversation.

I've seen couples thrive through this transition, and I've seen others struggle, and the difference often comes down to one simple thing...

Communication

Ask each other:

- What do we both want from the next chapter?
- How do we each imagine our days, our space, our travel, our time apart?

- What gives each of us energy, and what drains it?
- Where do our visions overlap and where might they clash?
- What should we consider doing together, and what might we want to consider doing apart?

My experience tells me that healthy couples in the 'what happens next' chapter of your life plan not only focus on their finances together, but also their time together and time apart.

It's not selfish to carve out individual pursuits; it's essential. Even the closest couples need separate sources of meaning.

So start with open, curious, non-defensive dialogue. Make it ongoing. Keep asking: 'How's this working for us?'

And remember that 'help' doesn't just come from experts. Sometimes the greatest help is sitting right next to you.

Your Financial Planner

Throughout this book we've concluded that money is a tool, which allows us to live the lives we want. Money is the hygiene factor, but a vital one which needs to be explored.

Across my career, I've met many people who've worked incredibly hard for decades, yet still feel anxious about whether they've got 'enough'.

Enough for what, though?

That's the question a good financial planner helps you define.

A great planner doesn't just crunch numbers; they act as a *thinking partner*. They help you translate your life goals into a financial roadmap.

They'll show you how long your resources might last, model different scenarios, and clarify trade-offs. The best financial planners I know will also help you see your money story. *How* beliefs you learned decades ago might be shaping decisions today.

And crucially, they help you feel confident that your finances can support your version of a life well lived.

When choosing a planner, I'd look for three things: competence, compatibility and clarity.

- Competence is how knowledgeable and skilful your financial planner is with the gold standard technical qualification being chartered, certified or both.
- Compatibility is about the relationship you have with your adviser. This should be a relationship of trust and confidence and ultimately is about how you get on with the person you choose.
- Clarity is the adviser's ability to explain specific concepts but also use tools like lifetime cash-flow models which can help you see the big picture.

Next You Might Want to Consider Adding a Coach to Your Team

If financial planners deal with the numbers, coaches help with the narrative.

Retirement isn't simply stopping work; it's redefining identity. Many of us underestimate how tied our sense of purpose is to what we do.

The challenge many of us face about asking friends is that often you get their opinion on what you should do, not the headspace to decide for yourself, although I suppose it depends on your friends!

A coach should give you the space to think, and the ability to ask challenging but insightful questions that allows you to define your 'what happens next' as well as possible.

They'll ask the questions most friends won't. What do you want to contribute now? What excites you? What fears are holding you back?

Coaches specialise in helping people design fulfilling post-work lives, balancing purpose, relationships, and wellbeing. They act as a sounding board, accountability partner, and occasionally, gentle challenger.

Working with a coach can help you clarify your values and priorities, explore possibilities you hadn't considered, design experiments to test new directions, and build routines that replace the structure work once provided.

And while coaching can feel like a luxury, for many it's a life-defining investment. You probably don't need coaching sessions forever, but sometimes just a handful of focused conversations can reframe your entire path.

I'd Also Suggest You Consider, Depending on Your Situation, Having a Few More Professionals on Your Team.

If you own a business or have complex finances, the transition to 'what's next' isn't just emotional, it's also technical.

A good solicitor helps you protect what you've built by drafting wills, powers of attorney, or shareholder agreements that reflect your current reality, not the one from ten years ago, as long as the legal side of business sales or employment changes.

An accountant ensures your transition is tax-efficient, especially if you're selling a business, accessing pensions, or restructuring assets.

Too often, people wait until a transaction is imminent before involving them.

The better approach is to be proactive. I'd start those conversations three to five years before you plan to make major changes. In my experience, the best way to achieve this is to align everyone at the same time, such as your financial planner, lawyer and accountant.

Finally, the Next Person You Might Want to Talk With About This Transition is Someone Who Has Already Gone Through it.

You want to pick somebody with a few similarities to you who's a few steps ahead.

It might be a colleague who semi-retired successfully, a friend who reinvented themselves, or someone you met on a walking holiday who found new purpose volunteering.

Ask them what surprised them, what they wish they'd known, what they'd do differently. Their experience can be a powerful shortcut through trial and error.

We underestimate how generous people can be with their wisdom when we simply ask.

It's also worth remembering. You can learn as much from the missteps of others as from their wins. Both offer valuable data for your own experiments.

Get Help Before it Gets Hard

Let's be honest, asking for help can feel uncomfortable.

Many of us spent decades being in charge. We led teams, raised families, ran organisations.

We're used to being competent, capable, and in control. So admitting we don't have all the answers can feel like failure.

But it isn't. It's just another stage of growth.

The philosopher Epictetus wrote, 'No great thing is created suddenly.'

Change takes time, but getting the right help can accelerate the time it takes to make some of these important decisions.

It's also important to remember that getting help doesn't make you less independent. I'd suggest it makes you more effective.

And often, the very act of reaching out to get help, making that call, booking that meeting, or joining that group becomes the first small experiment of your next chapter.

The modern myth of independence, that we should have it all figured out, might be one of the biggest barriers to wellbeing in later life.

The opposite of independence isn't dependence; it's interdependence. It's recognising that we flourish through connection.

Every person you bring into your 'what happens next' team adds another layer of wisdom, accountability, and encouragement.

And like many great designs, collaboration makes it better.

So Who Needs to Be on Your Team?

You might decide you only need to engage with your partner. Or that a partner, mentor, and coach will be enough to support you. You might choose to work with only your partner, your financial planner, and a team of professional advisers. That's up to you.

However, the message often repeated in this book remains.

Take a small, incremental risk-free action to start you off. Send a message. Book a coffee. Ask a question.

Each of those actions is a micro-step towards clarity and momentum remembering that your next phase isn't about finding one big answer.

It's about weaving together small conversations, small actions, and small experiments that accumulate into a life that feels more aligned, more energised, and more yours.

As we've explored throughout this book, working out what happens next isn't about following a set formula. It's about learning to listen more closely to yourself. It's about weaving together purpose, wellbeing, money, relationships, and time into something that feels unmistakably *yours*.

And yet, for all the planning, reflection, frameworks, and experiments, there comes a point where the thinking must become doing. A moment where the map stops being a drawing and starts becoming a journey.

A moment where we need to take some action.

That moment is now.

So let's take a look at everything we've covered so far. The stories, the science, the philosophy, the insights from brilliant guests, the practical tools, and all the lessons earned from decades of conversations with clients and bring them together.

Chapter Eleven

Your 'What Happens Next' Starts Today

'If you want to go fast, gone alone.
If you want to go far, go together.' – African Proverb

I'd love to tell you that Mike's story ends with a happily ever after.

I'd love to tell you that Mike found his purpose and now has the perfect balance of wellbeing in his life.

However, if I told you that it would be a lie. Mike still sends me photos of model aeroplanes, but when we meet now, we also talk about the work that's more meaningful for Mike, as well as the rowing machine in his gym, the art class he joined, and the people he's met along the way.

In reality, there's no perfect 'what happens next' chapter. There isn't for Mike, there won't be for me, and it's quite likely there won't be for you.

However, we can all take small incremental action – starting today toward a life we truly want to live. However, here's the truth...

No One is Going to Do This for You

Others can support you, advise you, open doors, remind you of your strengths, show you new paths, but the decision to step into your next chapter starts today. And it's *yours*.

Over the course of this book, we've explored the building blocks of a well-lived next chapter. Purpose, identity, values, financial confidence, physical vitality, social connection, intellectual and occupational curiosity, community, and stacking behaviours that make everything easier.

We've looked at models designed to help you find structure when we feel stuck between 'I know something needs to change' and 'I know what I'm doing next.'

You've also hopefully reflected on what enough means to you, what matters most, and what makes you feel alive.

But now we turn to the most important question of all:

- What will you actually do next?
- And just as importantly...
- When will you start?

The truth is, no one ever feels entirely ready. People don't change because the timing is perfect. Often they change because the cost of staying the same finally becomes harder than the cost of doing something different.

If you've reached this chapter, then that moment has already begun.

So with a deep desire for you to take that incremental next step, there's only one more question to ask.

For You... What Happens Next?

About the Author

Chris believes that good financial planning should have one simple purpose: to help people achieve their financial goals so they can live the life they want.

For Chris's clients, this involves building a plan that, over the long-term, helps them get from where they are today to what they want to achieve tomorrow and beyond. Chris is a chartered financial planner and one of the directors of Cervello Financial Planning. He is responsible for the strategic direction of the business, as well as continuing to look after his portfolio of clients. Chris is a fellow of the Personal Financial Society. Fellowship is the highest and most prestigious level of professional achievement is possible within the PFS.

Chris feels he's learned a lot as a financial planner in his twenty years of working with clients. He also believes in a consistent focus on improvement (something he tries to teach his daughters Sophie and Charlotte).

However, Chris also believes the true test of good financial planning is what clients say about the experience. That's why he's really pleased when his clients tell him they 'sleep better at night knowing that Chris and his team manage their wealth and support their financial goals'.

Chris has been fortunate enough to win several awards and has published two books, one helping employers comply with pension regulations and another sharing the stories of kindness he's collected while hosting a podcast with his daughter.

www.ingramcontent.com/pod-product-compliance
Lightning Source LLC
LaVergne TN
LVHW022055200926
848481LV00003B/924
9781918097726